THE NEW

BRYANT AND STRATTON

COMMON SCHOOL BOOK-KEEPING:

EMBRACING

SINGLE AND DOUBLE ENTRY,

AND

ADAPTED TO INDIVIDUAL AND CLASS INSTRUCTION IN SCHOOLS AND ACADEMIES.

By S. S. PACKARD,

PROPRIETOR OF PACKARD'S NEW YORK BUSINESS COLLEGE,

AND

H. B. BRYANT,

FOUNDER OF THE BRYANT & STRATTON CHAIN OF BUSINESS COLLEGES.

NEW YORK .:. CINCINNATI .:. CHICAGO

AMERICAN BOOK COMPANY

FROM THE PRESS OF
IVISON, BLAKEMAN & COMPANY

PREFACE.

THIS little book, almost in its entirety, was prepared and published more than seventeen years ago; and it is not too much to say for it that during the intervening time it has fairly divided with other works on this subject the growing patronage of public and private schools throughout the country.

That it has answered the purposes which called it into existence is evident, not only in the increasing demand for it, but more pointedly in the almost universal testimony of those best qualified to speak, viz.: the teachers who have used and are now using it as a text-book. Before undertaking the revision, its principal author communicated with a large number of this class, asking for criticisms and suggestions, and especially desiring to know if any radical changes as to matter or arrangement were desirable. The uniform reply has been that no such changes would add to the efficiency of the work, while they might cause more or less derangement and confusion in the large schools and classes now using the book. Of course, the last consideration would have little weight by itself, but if the changes, which might easily have been made, and which, under the plea of novelty and freshness, there was great temptation to make, would be likely to result in no real advantage, then the force of the argument must be recognized. But the author—much as he respects and would defer to the judgment of teachers who are, and are to be his patrons—could not afford to act in this matter contrary to his own convictions. A deference to the opinions of others may be a graceful and proper tribute to the wisdom supposed to exist in "a multitude of counsel," but an author can show no greater respect for this wisdom than to follow strictly the lead of his own well-founded convictions. And it may safely be assumed that the practice and experience of seventeen years' close attention to the study and appliances of the subject covered in this treatise has not left him without these well-founded convictions. And that they have a full expression in the aspect of the revised book as here presented may also be assumed.

A work of this scope does not require, nor should it have an elaborate philosophical statement of principles at the outset; nor should the plain, practical lessons which are its substance be environed with fine-spun theories or nicely-shaded definitions, which belong rather to the esthetics of logic than to the sharp enforcement of primal facts. The purpose of this book is to teach the practical lessons of Book-keeping; and its plan is to accomplish this in the most direct and positive way.

To that end, before taking up the science of Accounts as enforced in ble Entry Book-keeping, a proper space is given to the more simple,

3

because less comprehensive processes of Single Entry; so that the student may get hold of the instrumentalities of his work—technically, "learn the use of his tools," before he is called to the higher possibilities of their achievement. In Single Entry the form, as well as the use of personal accounts is clearly exhibited, and many of the foundation principles of the science of Book-keeping are illustrated; and not only the characteristics of the Ledger, but the utility of auxiliary books, and their substitution for the ordinary books of original entry are carefully exhibited. In fact, that part of the book has found particular favor in the eyes of intelligent teachers. The use of the same material for Double Entry and Single Entry—as in the case of Set 3—has afforded a most satisfactory means of distinguishing between the processes of the two methods.

The enforcement of the principles of Double Entry in Part II is made with as much point and conciseness as the author could command. Nothing essential has been omitted, and no redundancy practiced. The classification of accounts differs from the former edition only in its nomenclature, which is thought to be an improvement, simply because it is more clearly the expression of the real distinction in accounts.

In the regular order of the book, the plan has been to follow each fully-elaborated set with "Practical Exercises," in which the material only is given—in the shape of memorandum transactions—from which the student is required to write up, circumstantially, all the required books of entry after the preceding models. The good results which have followed this plan have suggested to the author the propriety of furnishing similar memoranda for the written sets; and inasmuch as it is deemed best to preserve the same order of arrangement as to consecutive pages, the desired memoranda, with such other material as the revision seemed to demand, will be found in the Appendix. It will be well if the student is required to use these memoranda strictly, in writing up the regular sets, rather than to copy from the book. The material for short sets given in the Appendix is to meet the expressed and proper demand of teachers who have felt the need of more frequent tests of their pupils' progress. There are decided advantages in reasonably long sets—and as a matter of drill they cannot profitably be omitted; but mere routine may be carried too far, and the pupil's mind thus diverted from the application of principles which is the main purpose of teaching.

But, after all, it is not presumed that any text-book is to supply that part of the work of instruction that belongs to the living teacher. A text-book is, at best, what its name implies, a book of texts, the elaboration, amplification and application of which depends wholly upon the teacher; and it would be saying too much for any text-book—as well as too little for the teacher—to assume that it should cover all the requirements of individual instruction, even in its material and suggestions.

There is at least no such claim for this book: the best it can hope to do is to serve as a convenient aid to teachers who will supplement its lessons and vary its methods to suit individual demands and answer a good conscience i the honest discharge of duty.

CONTENTS.

CONTENTS.

PART II.—DOUBLE ENTRY.

ABBREVIATIONS AND CHARACTERS

USED IN THIS BOOK.

ABBREVIATIONS.

A
Ac't. . . . Account.
Am't. . . . Amount.
Ans. . . . Answer.
Apr. . . . April.
Ass't'd. . . Assorted.
Aug. . . . August.

B
Bal. . . . . Balance.
B. B. . . . Bill Book.
brls. . . . . Barrels.
B. Pay. . . Bills Payable.
B. Rec. . . Bills Receivable.
Blk. . . . . Black.
Bo't. . . . Bought.
Bro't. . . . Brought.
B. W. . . . Black Walnut.

C
Cap. . . . Capital.
C. B. . . . Cash Book.
Co. . . . . Company.
Com. . . . Commission.
Const. . . . Consignment.
Cr. . . . . Creditor.

D
Dec. . . . . December.
D'ft. . . . Draft.
do. . . . . The same.
doz. . . . . Dozen.
Dr. . . . . Debtor.
d's. . . . . Days.

E
ea. . . . . Each.
E. E. . . . Errors Excepted.
Emb'd. . . Embroidered.
Ex. . . . . Example.
Exch. . . . Exchange.
Exp. . . . Expenses.

F
fav. . . . . Favor.
Feb. . . . . February.
Fig'd. . . Figured.
Fol. . . . . Folio.
For'd. . . . Forward.
Fr't. . . . Freight.

G
gcl. . . . . Gallon.

H
hhd. . . . . Hogshead.

I
I. B. . . . . Invoice Book.
Ins. . . . . Insurance.
Inst. . . . . Instant.
Int. . . . . Interest.
Inv. . . . . Invoice.
Inv't. . . . Inventory.

J
Jan. . . . January.

L
lbs. . . . . Pounds.
L. F. . . . Ledger Folio.

M
Mar. . . . . March.
Mdse. . . . Merchandise.
mo. . . . . Month.
Mgy. . . . . Mahogany.

N
No. . . . . Number.
Nov. . . . . November.

O
Oct. . . . . October.
O. I. B. . . Outward Invoice [Book.

P
p. . . . . . Page.
Pay't . . . Payment.
P. C. B. . . Petty Cash Book.
Pd. . . . . Paid.
Pkg. . . . . Package.
pr. . . . . Pair.
per. . . . . By.
Prem. . . . Premium.

R
Rec'd . . . Received.
R. W. . . . Rosewood.

S
S. B. . . . . Sales Book.
Sept. . . . September.
Ship't . . . Shipment.
Sunds. . . . Sundries.

Y
yds. . . . . Yards.
yr. . . . . . Year.

CHARACTERS.

@ . . . At.
% . . . Account.
% . . . Per Cent.
$ . . . Dollars.
¢ . . . Cents.

£ . . . Pound Sterling.
s . . . Shilling.
√ . . . Check Mark.
+ . . . Sign of Addition.
— . . . Sign of Subtraction.

× . . Sign of Multiplication.
= . . Sign of Equality.
1^1 . . One and one-fourth.
1^2 . . One and one-half.
1^3 . . One and three-fourth.

7

PLAN.

THE book is divided into two parts; Part I. is devoted to Single Entry, and Part II. to Double Entry. Each part has eight distinct series of transactions, comprising eight complete sets of books: four of which are written out in full—the other four given in the form of memoranda for the student to arrange after the models given.

In Part I., the *first* written set illustrates only the use of the main books, Day-Book and Ledger; the *second* set exhibits results; Set III. begins with a capital, representing a general merchandise business, shows the use of auxiliary books, and enforces the theory of loss and gain, by comparing the capital at beginning with that at closing. Set IV. represents a furniture business, introducing principal and auxiliary books.

In Part II., the *first* set is introductory, used to enforce the leading principles of the science; Set II. continues the business begun by Set I., enlarging the field and giving a wider scope of transactions—at the same time more fully presenting the theory and processes of Double Entry. This set is given in colors, as affording a better model for the student. Set III. contains the same material as the corresponding set in Part I., and is used principally to show the differences between Single and Double Entry. Set IV. is a practical set, using all the books of original entry as principal books—posting from them to the Ledger, and dispensing with the Journal, except for such entries as cannot properly appear in the other books. This set presents the economic methods of Double Entry.

The intermediate Examples for Practice and Practical Exercises explain themselves.

PART I.

SINGLE ENTRY.

PART I.

SINGLE ENTRY.

INTRODUCTION.

In getting at the true basis of a science, it is well, if possible, to follow the line of its history, and become familiar with the order and processes of its development. This is especially true of Book-keeping, for although it is purely a branch of mathematics, and as such entitled to the favor and consideration of scientific men, yet at no period of its history has it ranked in the estimation of scholars, with the more complex and abstract sciences. It is lamentably true that men will grow enthusiastic over the solution of a problem in Euclid, or the effect of a combination of movements upon a chess-board, who are ignorant of the first principles of this the most beautiful and practical of sciences; and are content to pass through life, receiving and appropriating the reputation belonging to men of science and erudition, while they are consciously unable to decide the simplest question in partnership settlements, or to appreciate the theory of debits and credits which lie at the basis of Book-keeping.

It is difficult to account for these facts except upon the ground that Book-keeping is too practical a science, and has too much "the smell of the shop." Whatever the reasons may be, the fact is that not enough interest has been felt in the subject to trace its history, which, therefore, must be inferred rather than compiled.

The prime condition of life is *want*, and the plans and purposes of life aim at supplying want. This necessity begets industry and frugality, and lays the foundation of progress in arts and civilization.

To supply the necessities of life the earth, through toil, is made to yield her abundance, and the various channels of enterprise and skill are laid open.

The wants of man are so numerous, and the means of supplying them so various, that a system of mutual dependence and reciprocal labor becomes not only economical, but essential; and thus, from the very beginning of human economy has there existed the necessity of a division and classification of labor and wealth.

The farmer, whose products supply hunger; the manufacturer of fabrics which are to clothe the body; the artificer, whose workmanship gratifies the more refined wants; the man of science, who contributes to the mind; the spiritual teacher, who ministers to the higher moral faculties, and the common laborer, who does the drudgery of life, are each dependent upon all the others for the sum of material and intellectual comforts which minister to their wants; and a mutual *exchange* of these comforts constitutes the foundation principle and impulse of the system of economy which we call BUSINESS.

To facilitate these exchanges it is found necessary to establish some standard of value by which the relative worth of commodities and services may be adjusted. The standard accepted by most civilized nations is gold and silver, which are coined in convenient particles and become the medium of exchange.

The particular necessity of Book-keeping is to preserve a record of such exchanges as would otherwise be trusted to memory; although its ultimate purpose embraces other important results. Its simpler purposes are here shown.

For example, John Smith is a farmer, and Thomas Jones a manufacturer; John raises as much food on his farm as is necessary to supply his own wants and those of his neighbor, while Thomas makes clothing sufficient for the demands of both. It is now the easiest thing in the world for both John and Thomas to have food and clothing, simply by exchanging with each other their surplus products. An exchange of this kind would need no record; and were this the extent to which commerce had been carried, it is not likely that obstinate brains would have been puzzled with the dry formulas of Book-keeping. But suppose, further, that Thomas should happen to be in *immediate* want of some of his neighbor's surplus food, without the ability, *at the time*, to render an equivalent in his own products. He says to John, "I want food, and cannot pay for it now, but if you will trust me, I will return you an equivalent when I have completed work now in progress." The conditions being satisfactory, the *food* is conveyed from John to Thomas, and the *promise* from Thomas to John. If John is blessed with a faithful memory he may be able to retain the facts connected with this transaction, and thus constantly bear in mind that he *owns* a certain quantity of clothing, which his neighbor is to bring him at a stated time. But suppose he is not willing to trust to his own memory, nor to that of his neighbor, but desires something tangible which shall at least *represent* this prospective property—a *record* which will not fade with the memory, but will stand for the benefit of whom it may concern, even in the absence of those having a personal knowledge of the facts. The person relied upon to fulfill this promise is Thomas Jones, and the most natural form of record would be to write his *name* in a book kept for that purpose, and state the fact underneath it, thus:

THOMAS JONES.

Bought of JOHN SMITH, a quantity of food, valued at *Ten Dollars*, for which he agrees to pay a quantity of clothing of equal value, on [naming the date of payment.]

A record like the above would be intelligible as containing all the facts, and affording to John Smith a tangible evidence of property which he owns, but which is in the hands of another party; and if this single transaction comprised all of this nature it would scarcely be worth while to attempt a more concise or symmetrical record. But as dealings of this kind may be very frequent, not only with Thomas Jones, but with other parties, it may be well to ascertain if some more satisfactory and less cumbrous method may not be adopted.

The simple fact expressed in the foregoing record is that Thomas Jones *owes* John Smith ten dollars worth of clothing. The only events which can vary this fact are, the payment of the debt, or a part of it, overpaying it, or adding to it by subsequent purchase without payment. There are, really, but *two* conditions, as pertaining to persons with whom we have dealings on credit, viz.: that of *owing*, and *being owed*. These two conditions are exact counterparts, and so far as they are equal, will cancel each other.

It will therefore be easy to arrange these opposite facts under the names to which they pertain in such way as that not only the facts themselves, but their relative results, may be ascertained at a glance. For example:

Dr.		Thomas Jones.						*Cr.*	
Date.		*He owes us.*	*Dol's.*	*Cts.*	*Date.*		*We owe him.*	*Dolls.*	*Cts.*
1878					1878				
Jan.	1	To 1 Bbl. Flour, . .	10		Jan.	15	By 4 yds. Cloth, . .	10	
Mar.	1	" 10 Bush. Wheat, .	12	50	Apr.	1	" Cash, ...	5	

This form has been found by experience to be both comprehensive and practical. It is called an *account*, and, as will be readily seen, is a statement of dealings with Thomas Jones. On one side are arranged the separate amounts of his indebtedness to us, and on the other of our indebtedness to him. The *difference* or *result* will be a net amount owing either to us from Thomas Jones, or to Thomas Jones from us. In other words, if Thomas Jones owes us more than we owe him, the indebtedness is in our favor, and may be reckoned as a part of our property; while, if we owe him more than he owes us, the indebtedness is in his favor, and should be reckoned among our debts. The facts shown in the account given may be thus analyzed: On the first of January Thomas Jones purchased of us 1 barrel of flour at $10; and on the 15th of January, sold us 4 yards of cloth for enough to cancel the debt. The amounts on the opposite sides of the account will now exactly balance each other, and the result is the same as though the exchange had been made at once. Again, on the first of March he purchased 10 bushels of wheat, for $12.50; and on the first of April pays us in cash $5. This leaves a deficiency in his account of the difference between $12.50 and $5;

14

and we say that Thomas Jones *owes* us $7.50. We have thus a tangible record of property, which if left to memory might be forgotten, and we thus become losers.

It will then appear that in all cases where exchanges are effected between parties, either of whom is allowed time to perform his part of the contract, some *written* record of the facts is necessary. This written record constitutes the germ of BOOK-KEEPING.

From the foregoing illustration it appears that an account has two sides, a *debtor* and a *creditor ;* that upon the debtor side is shown what is owing *to* us, and upon the creditor side, what is owing *by* us; that when the debtor side is the larger, the difference will express an amount belonging to us, and when the creditor side is the larger, the difference will express an amount which we owe. In the former case the account would represent property or resource ; and in the latter, debt or liability.

In the earlier history of Book-keeping, doubtless this form, or something similar, was deemed sufficient for the purposes of trade, it being absolutely necessary to have some written evidence only of such resources and liabilities as do not exist in tangible form, and which it would be unsafe to trust entirely to memory. It is evident, however, that in an extensive credit business, a book of *consecutive* record, giving a plain and simple account of the business as it progresses day by day, would be of essential service, and it is, therefore, the almost universal practice, particularly among merchants and tradesmen, to keep a Day-Book of some form, in which are written the transactions as they occur.

An example, showing one form of this book, and also that of the Ledger, with the transactions properly transferred, will be seen on the following page.

DAY-BOOK.

New York, January 30, 1878.

Jan.	30	JOHN SMITH,		*Dr.*	
		To 5 yds. Broadcloth........ @ $4 00	$20		
		" 10 do. Cassimere......... @ 1 50	15		
		" 30 do. Black Silk Dress.. @ 1 25	37 50		
		" 25 do. Flannel........... @ 50	12 50		
		" 10 do. Figured Silk..... @ 1 50	15	1 0 0	
Mar.	1	JOHN SMITH,		*Cr.*	
		By Cash paid on account,		7 5	

These entries, carried to the Ledger, which is the Book of Accounts, would appear thus:

LEDGER.

Dr. 　　　　　　John Smith. 　　　　　　 *Cr.*

Jan.	30	To Merchandise.....	1 0 0	Mar.	1	By Cash.............	7 5

The advantages of a Day-Book are twofold; first, it affords a regular daily history of the business; and next, by giving the particulars and details of each transaction in the Day-Book, the *amount* alone may be carried to the Ledger, requiring thus less space, and preserving a more symmetrical form of the Ledger accounts.

The Day-Book and Ledger in Single Entry contain only such transactions as relate to persons. All prudent men, however, will feel the importance of having a strict record kept of the receipts and payments of cash and other people's notes, and of the issue and redemption of their own notes. This is done by means of books specially arranged for such purpose.

The following are the most simple of these forms:

CASH BOOK.

			Received.		Paid.	
Jan.	1	Amount on hand, ...	3000			
		Received of James Monroe, on account, ...	150			
		Paid Store Expenses, as per Expense Book, ...			175	
		Lent John Thompson for one day, ...			500	
		Received of Jacob Schuyler for Bill of Mdse, ...	75			
		" " Robert M. Hart " " "	18	75		
		Paid A. T. Stewart in full of account, ...			400	
		Received for petty sales, as per Cash Drawer, ...	110			
		Balance on hand, ...			2278	75
			3353	75	3353	75
	2	Amount brought down, ...	2278	75		

BILL BOOK.

Bills Receivable.

No.	When Rec'd.	Drawer or Endorser	Drawee or Maker.	Date.	Time.	When Due.	Amount.	When and How disposed of.	
	1879.			1878		1879		1879	
1	Jan. 1	Rob't Minturn,	Jas. Cruikshank,	Dec. 1	60 ds.	Feb. 2	500	Feb. 2	Paid.
				1879					
2	" 5	Chas. Hawley,	David Woods,	Jan. 5	30 ds.	Feb. 7	1000	Feb. 7	Paid.
3	Feb. 1	Abram Duryea,	Duncan Phyfe,	" 10	90 ds.	Ap. 13	1500		
4	" 15	W. W. Granger,	Ivison & Phinney,	Feb. 15	60 ds.	Ap. 17	300		

Bills Payable.

No.	When Issued.	Drawer or Endorser.	Drawee or Maker.	Date.	Time.	When Due.	Amount.	When and How Redeemed.	
	1879.							1879	
1	Jan. 12	Sam'l Higgins,	Ourselves,	Jan. 12	15 da.	Jan. 30	150	Jan. 30	Paid.
2	Mar. 1	Peter Cook,	do	Mar. 1	90 da.	June 2	750		
3	" "	John D. Hinde,	do	" "	60 da.	May 3	300		

These simple and suggestive forms comprise the books commonly used in Single Entry; and are sufficient for the immediate demands of business record. However, they are but the preface of the multitudinous appliances which may be made useful in the various departments of business activity, and which, in some measure, will appear in the progressive steps of this little book.

QUESTIONS FOR REVIEW.

1. How can the true basis of any science be best estimated? 2. Why is this especially true of Book-keeping? 3. Why has Book-keeping not usually been ranked with abstract sciences? 4. What is the chief condition of life? 5. What does this necessity beget? 6. How are the necessities of life supplied? 7. What system grows out of the numerous wants of man? 8. Name some of the classes of men who are mutually dependent one upon the other? 9. What constitutes the foundation principle and impulse of business? 10. How are these exchanges facilitated? 11. How is the standard of value represented? 12. What is the particular necessity of Book-keeping? 13. In the case cited between John Smith and Thomas Jones, where the food and clothing are simultaneously exchanged, is there any actual need of a written record? 14. In the case where the payment of the clothing is deferred, why is a written record necessary? 15. What is the most natural record of the indebtedness of Thomas Jones in the example given? 16. Would this record be intelligible? 17. Why is a more symmetrical and concise record necessary? 18. What is the simple fact expressed in the foregoing record? 19. How may this fact be varied? 20. How many conditions are there pertaining to dealings with persons on credit? 21. How are these conditions as compared with each other? 22. How may these opposite facts be best arranged? 23. What is this form called? 24. How may it be defined? 25. What facts are arranged on either side of an account? 26. What is shown by the *difference* between the sides of an account? 27. Will you analyze the entries in Thomas Jones' account? 28. In cases where exchanges are effected involving *time* in their fulfilment, what is necessary? 29. What does this written record constitute? 30. How many sides has an account? 31. What are they called? 32. What is shown by the *debtor* side? 33. What by the *creditor* side? 34. If the debtor side be the larger, what will the difference express? 35. What, if the creditor side be the larger? 36. What will the account represent in the former case? 37. What, in the latter? 38. In the earlier history of Book-keeping what form of record was probably used? 39. Why was this form alone sufficient? 40. What other forms become necessary in an extensive credit business? 41. What book is usually kept by merchants and tradesmen? 42. What are the advantages of a Day Book? 43. What class of transactions do the Day Book and Ledger in a Single Entry contain? 44. What other records will all prudent men keep? 45. How is this done?

SET 1.—SINGLE ENTRY.

INTRODUCTORY.

DAY-BOOK AND LEDGER.

SHOWING THE USE OF THE BOOKS, WITHOUT EXHIBITING
A GENERAL RESULT.

REMARKS.

In the brief set which follows are given the simplest forms of Book-keeping—the Day-Book and Ledger. The purpose of the set is mainly to exhibit these books and their uses, in order that they may be fully understood in the uses to which they will hereafter be put.

The transactions which make up this Day-Book do not comprise the regular occurrences of a business, but only sufficient thereof to exhibit the form of entry;—hence no complete results are expected.

The Day-Book contains original entries of such sales and purchases as involve personal indebtedness, and of payments of cash or personal account. In fact, the Single Entry Day-Book and the Single Entry Ledger are used only to exhibit the facts of personal indebtedness. Any other information concerning the business must be gathered from other sources.

The form of the Day-Book is simple and direct, first giving the name of the person to be debited or credited, with the *fact* of "Dr." or "Cr.", and next, the detail of the purchase, sale or payment, with the final extension of the amount in the proper column.

The Student will first copy this Day-Book with much care, then post the items to the Ledger—indicating in the margin of the Day-Book the page or number of the Ledger account;—next, construct a Day-Book and Ledger of his own from the material in the Practical Exercises on page 26.

SINGLE ENTRY—DAY-BOOK.

New York, July 1, 1879.

1)	Robert Simpson,		Dr.		
	To 10 lbs. Rio Coffee,	@ 12¢	$1 20		
	1 ,, Best Black Tea,		1 00		
	25 ,, Crushed Sugar,	,, 12¢	3 00	5	20

,,

2)	James Cruikshank,		Dr.		
	To 1 box Raisins, 25 lbs.	@ 20¢		5	

,,

3)	Horace Webster,		Dr.		
	To 1 gal. Vinegar,		0 75		
	3 lbs. Black Tea,	@ 75¢	2 25		
	4 bush. Apples,	,, 1 00	4 00	7	

2

4)	W. L. Carpenter,		Dr.		
	To 50 lbs. Ham,	@ 11¢	5 50		
	1 box Herrings,		2 00	7	50
	Cr.				
	By Cash on ⁹/c,			5	

3

5)	John Shields,		Dr.		
	To 1 brl. Flour,			8	

,,

6)	Peter Van Wyck,		Dr.		
	To 5 gals. Cider Vinegar,	@ 75¢	3 75		
	3 bush. Potatoes,	,, 1 00	3 00	6	75

New York, July 5, 1879.

(7)	Peter Cooper,	Dr.				
	To 6 gals. Molasses,	@ 75¢	4	50		
	50 lbs. Sugar,	,, 12¢	6	00		
	12 ,, Coffee,	,, 11¢	1	32	11	82

—————— 6 ——————

(8)	Stephen Q. Hayward,	Dr.			
	To 1 bl. Mess Pork,		11	00	
	3 boxes Sugar, ea. 500 lbs. @ 6¢		90	00	101

—————— 7 ——————

(9)	J. B. Atwood,	Cr.		
	By bill of Merchandise, per Invoice,		300	
	——— Dr. ———			
	To order on S. Q. Hayward,		101	

—————— ,, ——————

(8)	S. Q. Hayward,	Cr.		
	By order, as above,		101	

—————— 8 ——————

(10)	James Sweeney,	Dr.			
	To 100 lbs. Loaf Sugar, @	9¢	9	00	
	50 ,, Crushed ,, ,,	8¢	4	00	
	3 hhds. Molasses, ,, $20		60	00	73

—————— 10 ——————

(11)	F. R. Stebbins,	Dr.		
	To 1 tierce Rice, 1800 lbs., @ 3¢		54	

1

Dr.   Robert Simpson.   Cr.

1879					
July	1	To Sundries,	1	5	20

2

Dr.   James Cruikshank.   Cr.

1879				
July	1	To 1 box Raisins	1	5

3

Dr.   Horace Webster.   Cr.

1879				
July	1	To Sundries,	1	7

4

Dr.   W. L. Carpenter.   Cr.

1879						1879				
July	2	To Sundries,	1	7	50	July	2	By Cash,	1	5

5

Dr. John Shields. Cr.

1879												
July	3	To 1 bbl. Flour,	1	8								

6

Dr. Peter Van Wyck. Cr.

1879												
July	3	To Sundries,	1	6	75							

7

Dr. Peter Cooper. Cr.

1879												
July	5	To Sundries,	2	11	82							

8

Dr. Stephen O. Hayward. Cr.

1879						1879				
July	6	To Sundries,	2	101		July	7	By ord. (Adv.)	2	101

9

Dr.　　　　　　J. B. Atwood.　　　　　　Cr.

1879					1879				
July	7	Ord. on Haywd.	2	101	July	7	By bill of Mdse	2	300

10

Dr.　　　　　　James Sweeny.　　　　　　Cr.

1879				
July	8	To Sundries,	2	73

11

Dr.　　　　　　F. R. Stebbins.　　　　　　Cr.

1879				
July	10	To 1 tierce Rice	2	54

PRACTICAL EXERCISES.

[To be written up after the manner of Set 1.]

TRANSACTIONS.—FIRST SERIES.

Jan. 1.—Sold J. L. Hunt, on %, 5 brls. Flour, @ $10 - - - - - - Sold C. E. Cady 25 lbs. Coffee, @ 10¢ ; 15 lbs. Oolong Tea, @ 75¢. Received cash on %, $10.

2.—Bought of W. H. Sadler, on %, 50 bush. Winter Apples, @ 50¢ ; 100 bush. "Early Rose" Potatoes, @ $2.50 - - - - - - Sold R. P. Dolbear, on %, 3 brls. Flour, @ $8.50.

3.—Sold L. L. Sprague, on %, 5 brls. "Pink Blow" Potatoes, @ $2.75 , 2 brls. Apples, @ $3.

4.—Paid W. H. Sadler, cash, on %, $100 - - - - - - Received of L. L. Sprague, cash, in full of %, $_____.

5.—Bought of B. F. Willson, on %, 5 brls. Mess Pork, @ $18.75.

6.—Sold Geo. Haley, on %, 2 brls. Mess Pork, @ $20 - - - - - - Sold Wallace P. Groom, on %, 10 lbs. Japanese Tea, @ 97¢ ; 100 lbs. Crushed Sugar, @ 12¢ ; 25 lbs. Mocha Coffee, @ 31¢.

8.—Sold G. E. Detwiller, on %, 3 firkins Prime State Butter, 210 lbs., @ 33¢. Received cash, on % of same, $50.

10.—Sold J. C. Miller, on %, 3 boxes Kendall's Laundry Soap, 283 lbs., @ 9¢.

11.—Received of Wallace P. Groom, cash, in full of %, $_____ - - - - Sold M. Hazzard, on %, 10 boxes Florida Oranges, @ $5.25.

12.—Paid W. H. Sadler, cash, on %, $100.

QUESTIONS.

1. What books are kept in Set 1 ?—*2.* What is the object of the Set ?—*3.* Are any complete results exhibited ?—*4.* What facts are presented in the Ledger ?—*5* What is the purpose of the Day-Book ?—*6.* What is the form of the Day-Book entry ?—*7.* What kind of information is contained in the Single Entry Day-Book and Ledger ?

SET 2.—SINGLE ENTRY.

RETAIL DRY GOODS BUSINESS.

DAY-BOOK, LEDGER, AND CASH-BOOK.

WITH STATEMENT OF FINAL RESULTS.

Prosperous.

REMARKS.

In this set we are enabled to arrive at more perfect and satisfactory results, and to carry out more fully the purpose of Bookkeeping—that of exhibiting, at any time, the condition of the business.

By the use of the Cash Book we compass a most important object, in keeping a check on the receipts and disbursements of cash, and showing the amount on hand. Of all the books used in business none is more essential than this; and no cautious business man will ever attempt to do without it. It is true, the amount of cash on hand may be easily ascertained at any time by *counting* it; but this process affords no test as to improper expenditures or omissions. A faithful record of the receipts and disbursements of cash, however—the difference agreeing with the amount actually on hand—gives a degree of confidence, not only in reference to the cash transactions, but to the business generally, which can be secured in no other manner.

A Cash Book, properly kept, will, at any time, show the amount of cash on hand; and for this purpose mainly is it introduced in this connection. The form here used, though perhaps not the best for general purposes, is extremely simple and easily understood. It is customary, in most business houses, to close up the Cash Book at the end of each business day, and bring the balance down as a basis for the next day's transactions. We have varied this plan to better suit our convenience, closing up each week during the first month's business, and only once in the next month. This is deemed sufficient for purposes of illustration.

The particular advance which is made in this set over the preceding is more apparent in the statement which follows the Cash Book, and which will show, at a glance, the real design of Bookkeeping.

Nothing is more desirable in connection with business record than the ability to exhibit *results* in a clear and unmistakable manner. To this end the learner should be taught to attach much importance to the *statements* given in connection with the various sets, and particularly to the principles deduced therefrom.

St. Louis, April 1, 1879.

(1)	Roberts, Rhodes & Co., (N. Y).			Cr.		
	By Mdse., per Invoice,				4000	
		"				
(2)	James Campbell,			Dr.		
	To 10 yds. Calico,	@	12¢	$1 20		
	5 ,, Ribbon,	,,	20¢	1 00		
	20 ,, Sheeting,	,,	10¢	2 00		
	5 ,, Broadcloth,	,,	3 00	15 00	19	20
		3				
(3)	Lauren G. Thomas,			Dr.		
	To 15 yds. Cassimere,	@	1 00	15 00		
	20 ,, Dress Silk,	,,	1 25	25 00	40	
		4				
(4)	R. B. Finney,			Dr.		
	To 10 yds. Vesting,	@	5 00	50 00		
	Trimmings, etc.,			10 00	60	
		5				
(5)	David P. Johnson,			Dr.		
	To 6 yds. Flannel,	@	- 50¢	3 00		
	12 ,, Alpaca,	,,	1 50	18 00	21	
		"				
(6)	Isaac Stevens,			Dr.		
	To 12 yds. Dress Silk,	@	1 50	18 00		
	6 ,, Fine Broadcloth,	,,	4 00	24 00	42	
		6				
(2)	James Campbell,			Cr.		
	By Cash on %,				10	

2

St. Louis, April 8, 1879.

(7)	Cyrus Wheelock,			Dr.		
	To 25 yds. 10-4 Sheeting,	@	75¢	18 75		
	6 pairs Ladies' Hose,	,,	1·00	6 00		
	12 yds. Printed Jaconets,	,,	15¢	1 80	26	55
	———— 10 ————					
(8)	Robert Demarest,			Dr.		
	To 25 yds. Black Doeskin,	@	2 00	50 00		
	50 ,, Bleached Shirting,	,,	15¢	7 50	57	50
	———— 12 ————					
(7)	Cyrus Wheelock,			Cr.		
	By Cash on %,				15	
	———— ,, ————					
(9)	James Atwater (per wife),			Dr.		
	To 1 doz. Linen Hdkfs.,			6 00		
	10 yds. Cotton Damask,	@	25¢	2 50		
	14 ,, Black Bombazine,	,,	1 50	21 00	29	50
	———— 15 ————					
(2)	James Campbell (per daughter),			Dr.		
	To 1 pair Lisle Gauntlets,			1 00		
	12 yds. French Calico,	@	15¢	1 80		
	3 doz. Satin Buttons,	,,	25¢	75		
	8 skeins Twist,	,,	4¢	32	3	87
	———— 16 ————					
(10)	James W. Lusk,			Dr.		
	To 1 yd. Black Satin,			2 00		
	Trimmings for Vest,			1 50	3	50

30

St. Louis, April 17, 1879.

(8)	Robert Demarest,	Cr.		
	By order on S. S. Packard, to Bal. ℀,		57	50
	"			
(11)	S. S. Packard,	Dr.		
	To order, as above,		57	50
	19			
(9)	James Atwater,	Dr.		
	To 20 yds. Linseys, @ 50¢	10 00		
	30 ,, Corset Jeans, ,, 30¢	9 00		
	1 doz. Gents. Socks,	3 00	22	
	20			
(11)	S. S. Packard,	Dr.		
	To 10 yds. French Broadcloth, @ 4 00	40 00		
	50 ,, Globe Drills, ,, 13¢	6 50		
	20 ,, Paper Cambrics, ,, 12¢	2 40		
	15 ,, Cotton Damask, ,, 25¢	3 75		
	30 ,, Cottonades, ,, 33¢	9 90		
	6 pairs Kid Gloves, ,, 75¢	4 50	67	05
	Cr.			
	By Cash,			50
(11)				

St. Louis, April 25, 1879.

(12)	John J. Howell, Jr.,			Dr.		
	To 10 yds. Mixed Satinet,	@	75¢	7 50		
	6 ,, Cotton Drilling,	,,	10¢	60		
	1 ,, Fine Satin,			2 00		
	10 skeins Twist,	,,	4¢	40	10	50

——————————— 27 ———————————

(13)	Amos Dean,			Dr.		
	To 6 yds Black Doeskin,	@	2 00	12 00		
	1 doz. Linen Hdkfs.,	,,	50¢	6 00		
	6 pairs Gents Hose,	,,	25¢	1 50	19	50

——————————— 30 ———————————

(9)	James Atwater,	Cr.		
	By Cash on %,		20	

——————————— '' ———————————

(3)	Lauren G. Thomas,	Cr.		
	By Cash in full of %,		40	

——————————— '' ———————————

(6)	Isaac Stevens,			Dr.		
	To 14 yds. Poplin,	@	1 25	17 50		
	1 pair Kid Gloves,			1 00	18	50

St. Louis, May 1, 1879.

(2)	James Campbell,		Dr.		
	To 12 yds. Brilliant,	@ 25¢	3 00		
	35 ,, Blk. Bombazine,	,, 1 50	52 50	55	50

2

(4)	R. B. Finney,		Dr.		
	To 10 yds. Blk. Doeskin,	@ 1 63	16 30		
	25 ,, Brown Sheetings,	,, 12¢	3 00		
	20 ,, Check Gingham,	,, 20¢	4 00	23	30

5

(1)	Roberts, Rhodes & Co.,		Dr.		
	To Cash (Dft. on New York), on %,			2000	

6

(11)	S. S. Packard,		Dr.		
	To 15 yds. Duck Drilling,	@ 20¢	3 00		
	10 ,, Brown ,,	,, 30¢	3 00		
	6 pairs Pearl Spun Hose,	,, 75¢	4 50	10	50

7

(5)	David P. Johnson,		Dr.		
	To 8 yds. Broadcloth,	@ 4 00	32 00		
	10 ,, Doeskin,	,, 2 00	20 00		
	1 ,, Satin,		2 00		
	Trimmings,		5 00	59	

,,

(8)	Robert Demarest,		Dr.		
	To 14 yds. Dress Silk,	@ 2 00		28	

St. Louis, May 9, 1879.

(14)	**Robert C. Spencer,**			Dr.		
	To 10 yds. Flannel,	@	50¢	5 00		
	6 Linen Hdkfs.,	,,	38¢	2 28		
	20 yds. Brown Sheetings,	,,	12¢	2 40	9	68

— 10 —

(6)	**Isaac Stevens,**	Cr.		
	By Cash on %,		30	

— 12 —

(4)	**R. B. Finney,**		Dr.		
	To 6 pairs Gents Hose,	@ 25¢	1 50		
	1 pair Suspenders,		1 00		
	1 ,, Kid Gloves,		75	3	25

— 15 —

(2)	**James Campbell,**		Dr.		
	To 10 yds. Broadcloth,	@ 4 00	40 00		
	6 ,, Doeskin,	,, 2 00	12 00	52	

— ,, —

(4)	**R. B. Finney,**	Cr.		
	By Cash on %,		25	

— 20 —

(12)	**John J. Howell, Jr.**	Dr.		
	To 4 yds. Beaver Cloth,	@ 3 00	12 00	
	1 ,, Satin,		4 00	
	Trimmings for Coat and Vest,		8 00	24

— 21 —

(7)	**Cyrus Wheelock,**	Cr.		
	By Cash in full of %,		11	55

St. Louis, May 25, 1879.

(4)	R. B. Finney,		Cr.		61	55
	By Cash to balance %,					

———————— 27 ————————

(12)	John J. Howell, Jr.,		Cr.			
	By 2 cords Wood,	@ 5 00	10 00			
	50 lbs. Butter,	„ 16¢	8 00	18		

———————— „ ————————

(10)	James W. Lusk,		Dr.			
	To 13 yds. Mous. de Laine,	@ 25¢	3 25			
	14 „ Figured Silk,	„ 1 50	21 00			
	Trimmings for Dress,		10 00	34	25

———————— 28 ————————

(14)	Robert C. Spencer,		Dr.			
	To 12 yds. Broadcloth,	@ 4 00	48 00			
	6 „ Black Doeskin,	„ 2 00	12 00	60		

———————— 30 ————————

(13)	Amos Dean,		Dr.			
	To 50 yds. Brown Sheeting,	@ 12¢	6 00			
	10 „ Pressed Flannel,	„ 75¢	7 50	13	50

———————— Cr. ————————

(13)	By Cash in full of %,				33	

A	N
Atwater, James, -------- 9	

B	O

C	P
Campbell, James, -------- 2	Packard, S. S., ---------- 11

D	Q
Demarest, Rob't, -------- 8	
Dean, Amos, ----------- 13	

E	R
	Roberts, Rhodes & Co., --- 1

F	S
Finney, R. B., ---------- 4	Stevens, Isaac, ---------- 6
	Spencer, Rob't C., ------- 14

G	T
	Thomas L. G., ---------- 3

H	U
Howell, I. I., Jr., ------ 12	

I J	V
Johnson, David P., ---- 5	

K	W
	Wheelock, Cyrus, ---------- 7

L	X Y
Lusk, James W., ------- 10	

M	Z

1

Dr. Roberts, Rhodes & Co. Cr.

1879						1879				
May	5	To Cash,	5/4	2000		Apr.	1	By Mdse.,	1	4000
								2000		

2

Dr. James Campbell. Cr.

1879							1879				
Apr.	1	To Mdse.,	1	19	20		Apr.	6	By Cash,	1	10
,,	15	,, ,,	2	3	87						
May	1	,, ,,	5/4	55	50						
,,	15	,, ,,	5	52							
		120 57		130	57						

3

Dr. Lauren G. Thomas. Cr.

1879						1879				
Apr.	3	To Mdse.,	1	40		Apr.	30	By Cash,	4	40

4

Dr. R. B. Finney. Cr.

1879							1879					
Apr.	4	To Mdse.,	1	60			May	15	By Cash,		25	
May	2	,, ,,	4	23	30		,,	25	,, ,,		61	55
,,	12	,, ,,	5	3	25							
				86	55						86	55

5

Dr.   *David P. Johnson.*   Cr.

1879										
Apr.	5	To Mdse.,	1	21						
May	7	,, ,,	5	59						
				80						

6

Dr.   *Isaac Stevens.*   Cr.

1879						1879				
Apr.	5	To Mdse.,	1	42		May	10	By Cash,	6	30
,,	30	,, ,,	4	18	50					
		30 50		60	50					

7

Dr.   *Cyrus Wheelock.*   Cr.

1879						1879					
Apr.	8	To Mdse.,	2	26	55	Apr.	12	By Cash,	2	15	
						May	21	,, ,,	6	11	55
				26	55					26	55

8

Dr.   *Robert Demarest.*   Cr.

1879						1879					
Apr.	10	To Mdse.,	2	57	50	Apr.	17	Order S. S. P.	3	57	50
May	7	,, ,,	5	28							
		28		85	50						

9

Dr.   James Atwater.   Cr.

1879						1879				
Apr.	12	To Mdse.,	2	29	50	Apr.	30	By Cash,	4	20
"	19	" "	3	22						
		31 50		51	50					

10

Dr.   James W. Lusk.   Cr.

1879										
Apr.	16	To Mdse.,	2	3	50					
May	27	" "	7	34	25					
				37	75					

11

Dr.   S. S. Packard.   Cr.

1879						1879				
Apr.	17	To D's order,	2	57	50	Apr.	20	By Cash,	3	50
"	20	To Mdse.,	3	67	05					
May	6	" "	4	10	50					
		85 05		135	05					

12

Dr.   John G. Howell, Jr.   Cr.

1879						1879				
Apr.	25	To Mdse.,	4	10	50	May	27	By Sundries,	7	18
May	20	" "	6	24						
		16 50		34	50					

13

Dr.   *Amos Dean.*   Cr.

1879						1879				
Apr.	27	To Mdse.	4	19	50	May	30	By Cash,		33
May	3	,, ,,	7	13	50					
				33						33

14

Dr.   *Robert C. Spencer.*   Cr.

1879										
May	9	To Mdse.	5	9	68					
,,	28	,, ,,	7	60						
				69	68					

Cash.

			Received.		Paid.	
1879 Apr.	1	Amount on hand,	1500			
		Paid for station'y, post. stamps, etc.			8	
		Received for petty sales this day,	115	25		
	2	Paid for insurance, ½% on $4000,			20	
		Paid drayage on Mdse.,			5	
		Received for petty sales this day,	175			
	3	Drew out for personal expenses,			15	
		Paid porter on % of wages,			5	
		Received for petty sales this day,	87	23		
	4	Paid expenses cleaning store,			2	50
		Paid for 1 box pens,				88
		Received for petty sales this day,	110	50		
	5	Paid for Letter press,			7	50
		Paid for putting light in window,			2	50
		Received for petty sales this day,	183	25		
	6	Received of James Campbell on %,	10			
		Paid clerk's salary,			15	
		Received for petty sales this day,	100			
		Balance on hand,			2199	85
			2281	23	2281	23
	8	Balance brought down,	2199	85		
		Paid for 1 doz. balls Twine,			1	20
		Paid for carriage hire,			4	
		Received for petty sales this day,	215			
	9	Paid for drayage, $4; porterage, $3,			7	
		Paid for show case,			20	
		Carried over,	2414	85	32	20

_____ *Cash.* _____

			Received.		Paid.	
1879						
Apr.	9	Brought over,	2414	85	32	20
		Received for petty sales this day,	76			
	10	Paid for Safe,			250	
		Paid book-keeper on %,			10	
		Paid small items of expense,			1	28
		Received for petty sales this day,	110			
	11	Paid rent in full to May 31,			200	
		Paid on bill of Furniture,			25	
		Received for petty sales this day,	76	75		
	12	Received of Cyrus Wheelock, on %,	15			
		Received for petty sales this day,	84			
	13	Received for petty sales this day,	98	75		
		Balance on hand,			2356	87
			2875	35	2875	35
	15	Balance brought down,	2356	87		
		Paid express charges,			1	50
		Paid for postage stamps,			1	
		Paid carpenter for repairing store,			56	83
		Received for petty sales this day,	95			
	16	Received for petty sales this day,	88	75		
	17	Received for petty sales this day,	126	31		
	18	Paid drayage, $4; freight, $7 50,			11	50
		Received for petty sales this day,	175			
	19	Received for petty sales this day,	210	50		
	20	Received of S. S. Packard on %,	50			
		Received for petty sales this day,	112	81		
		Balance on hand,			3144	41
			3215	24	3215	24

Cash.　　Received.　Paid.

			Received.		Paid.	
1879						
Apr.	22	Balance on hand,	3144	41		
		Paid for 2 tons Coal, @ $5 00,			10	
		Paid balance on Furniture,			53	
		Received for petty sales this day,	103	20		
	23	Received for petty sales this day,	129			
	24	Received for petty sales this day,	180	58		
	25	Paid book-keeper on %,			15	
		Received for petty sales this day,	98			
	26	Received for petty sales this day,	163	75		
	27	Paid for drayage,			10	
		Paid for porterage,			6	
		Received for petty sales this day,	173	81		
		Balance on hand,			3898	75
			3992	75	3992	75
	29	Balance brought down,	3898	75		
		Paid express charges on package from Chicago,			1	50
		Paid freight on Mdse.,			24	75
		Received for petty sales this day,	74	10		
	30	Received of James Atwater, on %,	20			
		Received of L. G. Thomas, in full,	40			
		Received for petty sales this day,	125			
		Balance on hand,			4131	60
			4157	85	4157	85

———— *Cash.* ———— Received. Paid.

1879			Received		Paid	
May	1	Balance on hand,	4131	60		
		Paid for firkin of Butter for family,			10	
	2	Paid for stationery,			1	50
	5	Paid Roberts, Rhodes & Co., on %,			2000	
	7	Paid clerk's salary,			50	
		Received for sales this week,	497	84		
	10	Received of Isaac Stevens, on %,	30			
	12	Paid for inv., Mdse., freight, etc.,			1575	88
		Paid on % of rent,			50	
		Paid for carriage hire,			15	
	14	Received for sales this week,	553	25		
	15	Received of R. B. Finney, on %,	25			
	17	Paid for ton of Hay,			12	
	20	Paid Gas bill,			10	24
	21	Received of Cyrus Wheelock, in full of %,	11	55		
		Received for sales this week,	723	85		
	25	Received of R. B. Finney, in full of %,	61	55		
	26	Paid for postage stamps,			3	
		Paid for stationery,			5	
	28	Received for sales this week,	573	24		
	30	Received of Amos Dean, in full of %,	33			
		Balance on hand,			2908	26
			6640	88	6640	88
		Balance on hand,	2908	26		

STATEMENT.

THE results of the foregoing record will be found condensed and classified in the statement which follows. A statement showing the condition of a business must of necessity exhibit its property and debts, or, as usually expressed, its *resources* and *liabilities*. The sources from which these facts are obtained in the present instance, so far as the record goes, are the Ledger and the Cash Book—the former giving the debts due to and from the concern, and the latter the amount of cash in possession. The value of unsold goods has to be obtained from actual inventory and appraisement, as is the case in any system of bookkeeping.

_____ Resources, or Property. _____				
1. *From Ledger Accounts.*—Balances due from persons.				
James Campbell, - - - - - - - - - -	120	57		
David P. Johnson, - - - - - - - - - -	80			
Isaac Stevens, - - - - - - - - - - -	30	50		
Robert Demarest, - - - - - - - - - -	28			
James Atwater, - - - - - - - - - - -	31	50		
James W. Lusk, - - - - - - - - - -	37	75		
S. S. Packard, - - - - - - - - - - -	85	05		
John J. Howell, Jr., - - - - - - - - -	16	50		
Robert C. Spencer, - - - - - - - - -	69	68		
2. *From Cash Book.*—Balance of Cash on hand, - -	2908	26		
3. *From Inventory.*—Merchandise on hand, - - -	1075	45	4483	26
_____ Liabilities, or Debts. _____				
From Ledger Accounts.—Balance due Roberts, Rhodes & Company, - - - - - - - -			2000	
Worth at the close, - - - - -			2483	26
Investment, - - - - - - - -			1500	
Net gain, - - - - -			983	26

45

DEDUCTIONS

From the foregoing analysis:

1.—To ascertain the NET CAPITAL *at any time.*
Subtract the sum of the liabilities from the sum of the resources.

2.—To ascertain the NET GAIN *during any period.*
Subtract the net worth at the beginning from the net worth at the close of such period.

[And by inference:—*1. To ascertain the* NET INSOLVENCY *at any time,* subtract the sum of the resources from the sum of the liabilities. *2. To ascertain the* NET LOSS *during any period,* subtract the net worth at the close from the net worth at the beginning of such period.]

EXAMPLES FOR PRACTICE.

[Let the student make out from these items written statements corresponding with that on the previous page.]

EXAMPLE I.—A merchant commenced business with a capital of $5000. At the end of the year he gathers from his books the following facts: Amount of Cash received, $15000 ; Amount paid out, $10500 ; A. B.'s account stands, Dr. $1500, Cr. $1000 ; C. D.'s, Dr. $4000, Cr. $3500 ; E. F.'s, Dr. $975, Cr. $450 ; G. H.'s, Dr. $483.75, Cr. $300 ; Merchandise on hand, as per inventory, $2750 ; Amount owing to J. K., $1500.

Required, the net capital at closing, and the net gain during business.

EXAMPLE II.—A. and B. commence business with the following resources: Cash, $3000 ; Notes, $1500 ; Merchandise, $3500 ; Real Estate, $10000 ; Balance due on personal accounts, $12500. At the end of six months, their resources and liabilities are as follows : Cash on hand, $1500 ; Cash in Bank, $4000 ; Notes, $3500 ; Merchandise, $3750 ; Real Estate, $15000 ; Due on Personal Accounts, $5000.—Amount due from the firm, on their notes, $750 ; Amount due to persons on account, $1500.

Required, the capital at commencing ; at closing ; and the net gain.

EXAMPLE III.—A merchant's capital at beginning is $3500. At the close of the period for which results are desired he has property and debts as follows :

Property.—Cash, $1575 ; J. L. Hunt's note, $3750 ; Merchandise, $4000 ; Due from persons, viz.: A. C. Lobeck, $150 ; Lottie Hill, $175 ; J. R. Bowman, $107.25 ; W. J. Maxwell, $315.

Debts.— Note favor Thomas Hunter, $1500 ; do. favor Henry Kiddle, $3000 ; Due on personal %, viz.: Rednor R. Wood, $750 ; Hugh Foulke, $375 ; W. E. Crocker, $1375.

Required, the capital at the close, and the net gain or loss.

PRACTICAL EXERCISES.

[To be written up as in Set 2.]

TRANSACTIONS.—SECOND SERIES.

July 1.—Commenced Business with Cash on hand, $1500 - - - - - Bo't of Harrison Scott, on %, 50 brls. Genesee Flour, @ $8 ; 2 hhds. Molasses, 140 gals., @ 40¢ ; 12 boxes Soap, @ $4 ; 6 half chests Y. H. Tea, @ $20 - - - - - Paid for stationery and sundry expenses, $50 - - - - - Rec'd Cash, for petty sales, $15.

2.—Sold J. W. Husted, on %, 10 brls. Genesee Flour, @ 9.25 ; 4 boxes Soap, @ $4.25 - - - - - Paid drayage, $2 - - - - - Rec'd Cash for petty sales, $50.

3.—Sold John Banks, on %, 15 brls. Flour, @ $9.50 ; 3 half chests Tea, @ $25 - - - - - Paid Harrison Scott, Cash on %, $200 - - - - - Rec'd Cash for petty sales, $75.

4.—Bo't of Henry P. Smith, on %, 10 hhds. Molasses, 1200 gals., @ 50¢ ; 12 boxes Havana Sugar, 3750 lbs., @ 6¢ - - - - - Sold J. C. Hall, on %, 10 gals. Molasses, @ 75¢. ; 1 brl. Flour, @ $9 - - - - - Rec'd Cash for petty sales, $110.

5.—Sold Henry P. Smith, on %, 5 brls. Flour, @ $9 - - - - - Rec'd Cash on %, of John Banks, $50 - - - - - Rec'd Cash for sales this day, $115.75.

6.—Paid Cash for stationery, $5.50 - - - - - Rec'd Cash for sales this day, $110.75.

8.—Bo't of C. J. Judd, on %, 5 brls. Coffee Sugar, 1000 lbs., @ 6½¢ ; 6 hhds. Molasses, 4000 gals., @ 50¢ - - - - - Rec'd Cash for sales this day, $75.50.

9.—Paid Cash for clerk hire, $50 - - - - - Rec'd for sales this day, $50.

10.—Rec'd Cash for sales this day, $83.30.

11.—Sold John Banks, on %, 10 gals. Molasses, @ 60¢ ; 50 lbs. Coffee Sugar, @ 7¢ ; 1 brl. Flour, @ $9 - - - - - Rec'd Cash for sales this day, $68.50.

12.—Paid C. J. Judd, Cash on %, $500 - - - - - Rec'd Cash for sales this day, $75.

13.—Rec'd Cash for sales this day, $117.50.

15.—Bo't of Thomas Palmer, on %, 3 brls. Soda Crackers, @ $4 20 ; 12 boxes Butter Crackers, 360 lbs., @ 6¢ ; 40 loaves Bread, @ 10¢ - - - - - Paid porterage in Cash, $3 ; For cleaning store, $5 - - - - - Rec'd Cash for sales this day, $123.75.

16.—Paid James Smith, Cash for repairing store, $25 - - - - - Sold Rob't Hayward, on %, 1 brl. Soda Crackers, @ $5 ; 3 boxes Butter Crackers, 90 lbs., @ 7¢ - - - - - - Rec'd Cash for sales this day, $97.50.

17.—Rec'd Cash for sales this day, $125.75.

18.—Sold W. F. Norman, on %, 100 lbs. Sugar, @ 7¢; 50 gals. Molasses, @ 60¢; 60 lbs. Sugar, @ 7¢ - - - - - - Paid Smith & McDougal for Printing Circulars, $5.50 - - - - - - Rec'd Cash for sales this day, $88.93.

19.—Paid Cash for postage stamps, $3; letter paper, $5 - - - - - Rec'd Cash for sales this day, $98.37.

20.—Rec'd Cash for sales this day, $117.95.

22.—Rec'd Cash, on %, of John Banks, $50 - - - - - Sold Robert Hayward, on %, 30 gals. Molasses, @ 60¢; 2 h'f chests Tea, @ $25 - - - - - Rec'd Cash for sales this day, $84.28.

23.—Rec'd Cash, on %, of Rob't Hayward, $30 - - - - - Rec'd Cash for sales this day, $75.

24.—Sold J. C. Buttre, on %, 1 hhd. Molasses, 75 gals., at 56¢ - - - - - Rec'd for sales this day, $65.75.

25.—Rec'd Cash of Rob't Hayward, in full of %, $49.30 - - - - - Rec'd Cash for sales this day, $78.25.

26.—Rec'd Cash for sales this day, $48.95.

27.—Paid clerk's salary in Cash, $50 - - - - - Rec'd Cash, on %, of J. C. Hall, $16.50 - - - - - Paid Henry P. Smith, Cash in full of %, $780 - - - - - Rec'd Cash for sales this day, $81.38 - - - - - Mdse. unsold, amounts, per inventory, to $1500.

QUESTIONS FOR REVIEW.

1. What more perfect results are shown in Set II. ?—*2.* What important end is accomplished in keeping a Cash Book ?—*3.* How may the amount of cash on hand be ascertained without the use of a Cash Book ?—*4.* What tests are omitted if we depend solely upon *counting* the cash ?—*5.* What advantages are there in a faithful record of receipts and disbursements of cash ?—*6.* What will be shown at any time by a Cash Book properly kept ?—*7.* How often in business is it customary to close up the Cash Book ?—*8.* How often is the Cash Book, used in this connection, closed ?—*9.* What is a desirable feature in business record ?—*10.* From what sources are the facts exhibited in the Statement on page 45 obtained ?—*11.* What is an indispensable requisite to any statement showing the condition of business ?—*12.* What is the rule for ascertaining the *present worth* of a concern ?—*13.* What, for ascertaining the *gain during business ?—14.* How may the *net insolvency* be found ? —*15.* How the *net loss ?*

Set 3.——Single Entry.

WHOLESALE DRY GOODS BUSINESS.

(PARTNERSHIP)

DAY-BOOK, LEDGER, SALES-BOOK, CASH-BOOK, AND BILL-BOOK.

WITH STATEMENT OF AFFAIRS AT BEGINNING, AND FINAL RESULTS.

Adverse.

REMARKS.

In this set we have enlarged the area of our work, first, by enlarging our business, and next by adding to the variety of the transactions. The feature of this set consists principally in the auxiliary books. The form of Cash Book here given differs from that in Set II. in its arrangement of receipts and payments. This form is the one in common use, and is better than the other, mainly on account of its complete separation of these two conditions; the *receipts* being placed on one page, and the *payments* on the other. The Bill Book and Sales Book will explain themselves. There are more comprehensive forms for the Bill Book in use, but the one here shown is the common form, and has the merit of simplicity and plainness. The Sales Book is an essential auxiliary for a merchant, particularly where any amount of wholesaling or general credit business is done. It is not really necessary that the credit sales should be entered on the Day Book, as they may easily be posted from the Sales Book direct; but as many merchants adopt the plan of posting *only* from the Day Book, and as there are some very good reasons for adopting this policy, we have here given it the preference. The initials, "D. B.," "C. B.," and "B. B.," in the margin of the Sales Book, (standing for Day Book, Cash Book, and Bill Book), will indicate the books wherein are entered the various resources received for merchandise. The Sales Book is not, properly speaking, a book of *results*, and is not consulted in making up our list of resources and liabilities.

In the former set the result of the business was a gain; in this a loss has been sustained, which is shared equally by the two partners.

In writing up this set let the student observe the order of dates in the various books, and complete the record of each transaction before proceeding to the next. For example: On the 1st of July, Robert Van Schaick purchased a bill of goods for which he paid cash. This entry is first made in the Sales Book, from which the amount is transferred to the Cash Book, and marked " C. B." in the margin of the Sales Book. The succeeding entries in the Sales Book are, in the same manner, transferred to the appropriate books which are indicated in the margin.

50

1)	H. B. Bryant,	Cr.		
	For investment in business, viz.:			
	Merchandise, as per inventory,		$4750	
	Notes, as per Bill Book,		1500	
	Cash, as per Cash Book,		1200	
	Balances due on personal accounts, viz.:			
	John R. Penn,		500	
	L. Fairbanks,		750	
	Alonzo Gaston,		375	9075
	"			
2)	H. D. Stratton,	Cr.		
	For investment, as follows:			
	House and Lot, valued at		5000	
	Cash in Union Bank,		3000	8000
	"			
3)	John R. Penn,	Dr.		
	To balance favor of H. B. Bryant,			500
	"			
4)	Lorenzo Fairbanks,	Dr.		
	To balance favor of H. B. Bryant,			750
	"			
5)	Alonzo Gaston,	Dr.		
	To balance favor of H. B. Bryant,			375

2

Albany, July 2, 1879.

(3)	John R. Penn,	Cr.		
	By Cash on %,		250	
	3			
(6)	James Johnson,	Dr.		
	To bill of Mdse. per Sales Book,		192	
	5			
(7)	Claflin, Mellen & Co. (N.Y.),	Cr.		
	By invoice Boots and Shoes,		575	
	"			
(8)	A. T. Stewart & Co.,	Cr.		
	By invoice Dry Goods,		757	
	7			
(9)	E. B. Rice,	Dr.		
	To bill of Mdse. per Sales Book,		42	45
	"			
(5)	Alonzo Gaston,	Cr.		
	By Cash in full of %,		375	
	10			
(10)	Benjamin Payn,	Dr.		
	To bill of Mdse. per Sales Book,		23	41
	"			
(8)	A. T. Stewart & Co.,	Dr.		
	To Cash on %,		300	

Albany, July 12, 1879.

(2)	H. D. Stratton, *Dr.*		
	To accepted draft, favor of P. R. Spencer, as per Bill Book,	75	
	13		
(11)	Amos Dean, *Dr.*		
	To bill of Mdse. per Sales Book,	180	
	15		
(7)	Claflin, Mellen & Co., *Dr.*		
	To note @ 60 ds., to balance %,	575	
	"		
(1)	H. B. Bryant, *Dr.*		
	To Cash on private %,	75	
	16		
(4)	Lorenzo Fairbanks, *Cr.*		
	By Cash on %,	350	
	20		
(12)	Victor M. Rice, *Dr.*		
	To bill of Mdse. per Sales Book,	82	88
	Cr.		
(12)	By Cash on %,	30	
	21		
(11)	Amos Dean, *Cr.*		
	By Cash on %,	50	
	23		
(13)	James Sheldon, *Dr.*		
	To bill of Mdse. per Sales Book,	132	24

Albany, July 24, 1879.

(2)	E. B. Rice,	Cr.		
	By Cash in full of %,		42	45

—————— 25 ——————

(14)	William Shepard,	Dr.		
	To bill of Mdse. per Sales Book,		37	55

—————— 26 ——————

(15)	John Belden.	Dr.		
	To bill of Mdse. per Sales Book,		216	50

—————— '' ——————

(5)	A. T. Stewart & Co.,	Dr.		
	To Cash in full of %,		457	

—————— 29 ——————

(3)	John R. Penn,	Cr.		
	By Cash in full of %,		250	

—————— 31 ——————

(16)	Charles A. Seeley,	Dr.		
	To Mdse. as per Sales Book,		182	40

—————— Cr. ——————

| (16) | By Cash on %, | | 75 | |

A	N
B	**O**
Bryant, H. B., --------- 1	
Belden, John, ----------- 15	
C	**P**
Claflin, Mellen & Co., ---- 7	Penn, John R., ---------- 3
	Payn, Benj., ----------- 10
D	**Q**
Dean, Amos, ----------- 11	
E	**R**
	Rice, E. B., ---------- 9
	Rice, V. M., ----------- 12
F	**S**
Fairbanks, Lorenzo, ------- 4	Stratton, H. D., -------- 2
	Stewart, H. J., & Co. --- 8
	Sheldon, James, --------- 13
	Shepard, William, -------- 14
	Seeley, Chas. H., ------- 16
G	**T**
Gaston, Alonzo, ----------- 5	
H	**U**
I J	**V**
Johnson, James, ----------- 6	
K	**W**
L	**X Y**
M	**Z**

1

Dr.   H. B. Bryant.   Cr.

1879 July	15	To Cash,	3	75	1879 July	1	By invest'd,	1	9075

2

Dr.   H. D. Stratton.   Cr.

1879 July	12	To Acceptance	3	75	1879 July	1	By invest'd,	1	8000

3

Dr.   John R. Penn.   Cr.

1879 July	1	Bal. H. B. B.	1	500	1879 July "	2 29	By Cash, " "	2 4	250 250
				500					500

4

Dr.   Lorenzo Fairbanks.   Cr.

1879 July	1	Bal. H. B. B.	1	750	1879 July	16	By Cash,	3	350

5

Dr.   Alonzo Gaston.   Cr.

1879					1879				
July	1	Bal. H.B.B.	1	375	July	7	By Cash,		375

6

Dr.   James Johnson.   Cr.

1879				
July	3	To Mdse.,	2	192

7

Dr.   Claflin, Mellen & Co.   Cr.

1879					1879				
July	15	To Note,	3	575	July	5	By Mdse.,	2	575

8

Dr.   A. T. Stewart & Co.   Cr.

1879					1879				
July	10	To Cash,	2	300	July	5	By Mdse.,	2	757
"	26	" "	4	457					
				757					757

57

9

Dr.   E. B. Rice.   Cr.

1879						1879					
July	7	To Mdse.,	2	42	45	July	24	By cash,	4	42	45

10

Dr.   Benjamin Payn.   Cr.

1879											
July	10	To Mdse.,	2	23	41						

11

Dr.   Amos Dean.   Cr.

1879						1879					
July	13	To Mdse.,	3	180		July	21	By cash,	3	50	

12

Dr.   Victor M. Rice.   Cr.

1879						1879					
July	20	To Mdse.,	3	82	88	July	20	By cash,		30	

13

Dr.   James Sheldon.   Cr.

1879								
July 23	To Mdse.,	3	132	24				

14

Dr.   William Shepard.   Cr.

1879								
July 25	To Mdse.,	4	37	55				

15

Dr.   John Belden.   Cr.

1879								
July 26	To Mdse.,	4	216	50				

16

Dr.   Charles A. Seeley.   Cr.

1879					1879			
July 31	To Mdse.,	4	182	40	July 31	By Cash,	4	75

Albany, July 1, 1879.

C.B.	**Robert Van Schaick,**			Cash.	
	110 yds. Merrimack Prints,	@ 11¢	$12 10		
	75 ,, Union ,,	,, 10¢	7 50		
	120 ,, Orange ,,.	,, 9½¢	11 40		
	80 ,, Lowell ,,	,, 10¢	8 00	39	00

3

D.B.	**James Johnson,**			On %.	
	2 cases Men's Thick Boots, 24 pr., @ $2,	$48 00		
	3 ,, Calf Welt ,, 36 ,, ,, 3,	108 00		
	1 ,, Boys' Grain D.S. ,, 12 ,, ,, 3,	36 00	192	

4

B.B.	**E. H. Bender,**			Note @ 60 ds.	
	1 case Pemb'n Rem'ts, 1200 yds. @ 5½¢	$66 00		
	9 pieces Lynn Cottons, 270 ,, ,, 11¢	29 70		
	3 ,, Scotch P. Ging. 125 ,, ,, 10¢	12 50	108	20

7

D.B.	**E. B. Rice,**			On %.	
	2 pieces Eagle Cottons, 80 yds., @ 12¢	$9 60		
	3 ,, Garibaldi Twills, 95 ,, ,, 9¢	8 55		
	2 ,, Bl'ch Drills, 90 ,, ,, 11¢	9 90		
	4 ,, Marietta Cloth, 120 ,, ,, 12¢	14 40	42	45

8

C.B.	**W. H. Clark,**			Cash	
	3 pieces Bar Muslin, 54 yds. @ 13¢	$7 02		
	2 ,, Brilliante, 64 ,, ,, 20¢	12 80	19	82

Albany, July 10, 1879.

D.B.	Benjamin Payn,			On %.		
	6 pieces Paper Cambric, 72 yds., @	8¢	$5 76			
	1 ,, 6-4 Cot. Dam., 36 ,, ,,	40¢	14 40			
	1 ,, Canvas, 25 ,, ,,	13¢	3 25	23	41	

————— 12 —————

B.B.	Calvin S. Sill (Troy),		Note @ 90 ds.			
	10 pieces Fancy Linen, 120 yds., @	25¢	$30 00			
	20 ,, Crash Linen, 200 ,, ,,	9¢	18 00			
	15 ,, Eng'h Prints, 200 ,, ,,	22¢	44 00			
	3 doz. Balmoral Skirts, 36 @ $2 25		81 00	173		

————— 13 —————

D.B.	Amos Dean,		On %.			
	3 cases Kip Brogans, 72 pr. @ $1 50		$108 00			
	2 ,, Ladies' Sand. 120 ,, ,,	60¢	72 00	180		

————— 18 —————

C.B.	Geo. H. Doty (Schenectady),		Cash.			
	2 cas. Wom. Walk. Shoes, 120 pr. @ $1 00		$120 00			
	1 ,, Lad. Mor. ,, 48 ,, ,, 1 50		72 00			
	4 pcs. Check Marseilles, 40 yds. ,, 75¢		30 00			
	10 ,, Cam. Curt. Cth., 120 ,, ,, 25¢		30 00	252		

————— 20 —————

D.B.	Victor M. Rice,		On %.			
	1 doz. Silk Scarfs, 12 @ 88¢		$10 56			
	4 pcs. English Tweed, 36 yds., ,, $1 12		40 32			
	2 ,, Span. Ch. Pts, 80 ,, ,, 40¢		32 00	82	88	

Albany, July 22, 1879.

B.B.	James R. Morgan (Buf.), Note @ 6 mos			
	3 doz. Elastic Hoop Skirts, 36 @ $2 50 $90 00			
	1 ,, Stella Shawls, 12 ,, 2 00 24 00			
	6 pcs. Parametta, 300 yds., ,, 75¢ 225 00	339	

23

D.B.	James Shelden (Schoharie), On %.			
	3 cases Congress Gaiters, 36 pr., @ $1 30 $46 80			
	4 ,, Jenny Lind ,, 48 ,, ,, 1 12 53 76			
	2 ,, Misses' Sandals, 96 ,, ,, 33¢ 31 68	132	24

,,

C.B.	Robert Metcalf, Cash.			
	4 cases Men's Thick Boots, 48 pr. @ $1 50 $72 00			
	3 ,, Calf Welt ,, 36 ,, ,, 2 00 72 00			
	1 ,, Patent Leath. ,, 12 ,, ,, 5 00 60 00			
	1 ,, Misses' School Shoes, 60 ,, ,, 50¢ 30 00	234	

24

C.B.	Charles Heydon (Greenbush), Cash.			
	1 piece Blk. Doeskin, 20 yds., @ $1 25 $25 00			
	3 pcs. Corset Jeans, 90 ,, ,, 10¢ 9 00			
	6 ,, Delaine, 180 ,, ,, 40¢ 72 00	106	

25

D.B.	William Shepard (Hudson). On %.			
	6 pcs. Lancas. Gingham, 250 yds. @ 10¢ $25 00			
	1 ,, Canvas, 30 ,, ,, 12½¢ 3 75			
	1 ,, Padding, 40 ,, ,, 10¢ 4 00			
	3 ,, Wiggin, 60 ,, ,, 8¢ 4 80	37	55

Albany, July 25, 1879.

C.B.	Rob't Dawes (Pittsfield, Ms.), Cash.			
	4 cases Misses' Fancy Ties, 96 pr. @ 70¢	$67 20		
	2 ,, Ankle Boots, 48 pr. @ $1 25	60 00		
	1 ,, Kid Gaiters, 24 ,, ,, 1 50	36 00	163 20	

— 26 —

D.B.	John Belden (Utica), On %.			
	2 pcs. Fancy Cassimeres, 50 yds. @ $1 25	$62 50		
	3 ,, Saco ,, 60 ,, ,, 1 00	60 00		
	9 ,, Hard Times ,, 270 ,, ,, 20¢	54 00		
	2 ,, Striped Satinet, 80 ,, ,, 50¢	40 00	216 50	

— 27 —

C.B.	James H. Lansley, Cash.			
	1 doz. Stella Shawls, 12 @ $2 00	$24 00		
	3 ,, Balmoral Skirts, 36 ,, 2 25	81 00		
	2 ,, Silk Scarfs, 24 ,, 88¢	21 12		
	3 ,, Gents. L. Hdkfs, 36 ,, 35¢	12 60	138 72	

— 29 —

C.B.	W. H. Figuet, (Marion, Ala.), Cash.			
	8 pcs. Turkey Red Prints, 200 yds. @ 16¢	$32 00		
	10 ,, English Tweed, 90 ,, ,, 1 00	90 00		
	2 ,, Spanish Check, 80 ,, ,, 40¢	32 00	154	

— 31 —

D.B.	Charles A. Seeley (Rochester), On %.			
	4 cas. Miss. Renfrew Boots, 96 pr. @ $1 00	$96 00		
	2 ,, Ladies' Rarey ,, 24 ,, ,, 2 00	48 00		
	2 ,, Miss. Union Gait., 48 ,, ,, 80¢	38 40	182 40	

1

Cash.   Receipts.

1879						
July	1	Am't invested by H. B. Bryant,	1200			
	,,	,, ,, ,, H. D. Stratton (in bank),	3000			
	,,	Rec'd for Mdse. sold Rob't Van Shaick,	39			
	2	on % of I. R. Penn,	250			
	3	for petty sales,	17	50		
	7	of Alonzo Gaston, in full of %,	375			
	8	,, W. H. Clark for Mdse. per S. B.	19	82		
	10	Amount of Rob't Bruce's note,	500			
	12	for petty sales,	33	50		
	16	of Lorenzo Fairbanks, on %,	350			
	18	G. H. Doty for Mdse. per S. B.,	252		6036	82
					6036	82
	18	Balance on hand,			5403	57
	20	Rec'd on % of Victor M. Rice,	30			
	21	,, ,, Amos Dean,	50			
	23	of R. Metcalf for Mdse. per S. B.	234			
	24	Cha's Heydon ,, ,, ,,	106			
	,,	E. B. Rice, in full of %,	42	45		
	25	Rob't Dawes,	163	20		
	27	I. H. Lansley for Mdse. per S. B.	138	72		
	29	W. H. Fiquet ,, ,,	154			
	,,	John R. Penn in full of %,	250			
	31	Cha's H. Seeley on %,	75		1243	37
					6646	94
		Balance on hand,			5881	94

————— Cash. —————

Payments.

1879							
July	1	Paid for postage stamps and pens.	5				
	2	,, printing hand bills,	10				
	4	C. Jones for repair. store (per ck.),	175				
	5	freight on Mdse. (per ck.),	27	50			
	7	clerk hire,	25				
	8	expenses to New York,	15	75			
	10	A. T. Stewart & Co., on %,	300				
	15	H. B. Bryant on private %,	75		633	25	
		Balance on hand,			5403	57	
					6036	82	
	19	Paid for advtst. in Eve. Journal,	15				
	20	,, petty expenses,	10				
	21	bill for carpenter work (per ck.),	175				
	,,	drayage, $5; postage, $3,	8				
	25	clerk hire,	25				
	,,	for accept. fav. of H. D. Stratton,	75				
	26	H. T. Stewart, in full of %,	457		765		
		Balance on hand,			5881	94	
					6646	94	

Bill - Book.

Receivable.

No.	When Rec'd.	For what Rec'd.	Drawer or Endorser.	Drawee or Maker.	Date.	Term.	When Due.	Amount.	When and How Disposed of.
	1879				1879		1879		1879
1	July 1	Invest. H. B. B.,	Henry Twison,	Robert Bruce,	June 7	30 ds.	July 10	500	July 10 Paid.
2	" 1	"	James W. Lusk,	S. S. Packard,	Jan. 10	8 mos.	Sept. 13	1000	
3	" 4	Mdse.,	F. T. Catkins,	E. H. Bendel,	July 4	60 ds.	" 5	108 20	
4	" 12	"	G. V. L. Quackenb'h,	Calvin S. Hill,	" 12	90 ds.	Oct. 13	173	
							1880		
5	" 22	"	W. P. Spencer,	James R. Morgan,	" 22	6 mos.	Jan. 25	339	

Payable.

No.	When Issued.	For what Issued.	Drawer or Endorser.	Drawee or Maker.	Date.	Term.	When Due.	Amount.	When and How Disposed of.
	1879				1879		1879		1879
1	July 12	H. D. S.	P. R. Spencer,	H. D. Stratton,	July 12	10 ds.	July 25	75	July 25 Paid.
2	" 15	To close %.	Claflin, Mellen & Co.	Bryant & Stratton,	" 15	60 ,,	Sept. 16	575	

STATEMENT

——— Resources. ———	Dr.		Cr.		Balance.	
1. *From Ledger Accounts:*						
Lorenzo Fairbanks, ...	750		350		400	
James Johnson, ...	192				192	
Benjamin Payn, ...	23	41			23	41
Amos Dean, ...	180		50		130	
Victor M. Rice, ...	82	88	30		52	88
James Sheldon, ...	132	24			132	24
William Shepard, ...	37	55			37	55
John Belden, ...	216	50			216	50
Chas. A. Seeley, ...	182	40	75		107	40
2. *From Cash Book:*						
Balance of Cash on hand, ...					5881	94
3. *From Bill Book:*						
S. S. Packard's Note, due Sept. 13, ...			$1000			
E. H. Bender's " " 5, ...			108	20		
Calvin S. Sill's " " Oct. 13, ...			173			
J. R. Morgan's " " Jan. 25, ...			339		1620	20
4. *From Inventory:*						
Merchandise unsold, ...					3000	
Real Estate, ...					5000	
					16794	12
——— **Liabilities.** ———						
From Bill Book:						
Note favor Claflin, Mellen & Co., ...					575	
Present Capital, ...					16219	12

To ascertain the net loss of the concern, and the present worth of each partner, we have the following facts:

H. B. Bryant invested, ...	$9075		
" drew out, ...	75		
Net investment, ...		$9000	
H. D. Stratton invested, ...	$8000		
" drew out, ...	75		
Net investment, ...		7925	
Total net investment, ...		$16925	
Deduct Present Worth, ...		16219	12
Leaves Net Loss, ...		$705	88
H. B. Bryant's original investment, ...	$9000		
Less ½ Net Loss, ...	352	94	
Leaves present investment, ...		£647	06
H. D. Stratton's original investment, ...	$7925		
Less ½ Net Loss, ...	352	94	
Leaves present investment, ...		7572	06
Total Present Capital, ...		$16219	12

67

From the foregoing statement we deduce the following

RULES.

1.—To ascertain the NET LOSS *during business, subtract the net capital at closing from the net capital at commencing.*

2.—To ascertain the NET CAPITAL *of each partner at closing, subtract his* NET LOSS *from, or add his* NET GAIN *to his* NET INVESTMENT.

EXAMPLES FOR PRACTICE.

EXAMPLE I.—A. commenced business with a cash capital of $8750. At the close of the year his resources and liabilities were as follows: Cash on hand, $3700; Notes on hand, $7000; Merchandise unsold, $2500; Amounts owing on Personal Accounts, $2000.— He owes on notes, $5000; To various persons, $2500.

What has been his loss? What is his net capital at closing?

EXAMPLE II.—E. and F. enter into copartnership on equal terms, each investing at commencement, $10000; and each withdrawing during the business, $1500. At the close of a certain period the following exhibit shows the true condition of their affairs: Cash on hand, $500; Balance in Bank, $7000; Due them on Personal Accounts, $5783.75, of which $875 is worthless; Due them on Notes, $6750; Merchandise on hand, $2700; Real Estate, $5000; Bank Stock, $3500. — They owe to persons on account, $10000; On Notes, $5600.

Have they gained or lost in business, and how much? What is each partner's net capital at closing?

EXAMPLE III.—A. B. and C. are partners. A. puts into the concern, $7500; B., $5300; C., $4700. At the close of the year their books exhibit the following results; John Smith, Dr. $1700, Cr. $500; John Parker, Dr. $1100, Cr. $975; Abram Schenck, Dr. $1750, Cr. $2700; Albert Dodge, Dr. $1859.38, Cr. $212.50; Cash received, $125386.29; Paid out, 122480.23; Notes received, $1900; Notes disposed of, $1200; Merchandise unsold, $2700; Value of Store and Fixtures, $15750; A. has drawn out $2000; B., $1500; C., $785.—They have issued Notes to the amount of $30000, of which they have redeemed $25800.

Required a written statement which shall exhibit all these facts, as also the amount of gain or loss during the business, and each partner's net capital at closing.

PRACTICAL EXERCISES.

[To be written up after the manner of Set 3.]

TRANSACTIONS.—THIRD SERIES.

July 1.—S. S. Packard and John R. Penn have engaged in a general merchandise business, the gains and losses of which they agree to share equally. S. S. Packard invests *Cash*, $4000; *Merchandise*, $1750; *Notes*, as follows: one for $500, in favor of S. S. P., signed by H. B. Bryant, and endorsed by W. P. Spencer, dated June 1, @ 60 ds.; and one for $700, an accepted draft, drawn by L. S. Bliss on George Claghorn, May 1, at 90 ds. sight, and accepted May 3; *Personal Accounts*, as follows: Henry Fish, $500; Robert Fulton, $750; David Coleman, $900. John R. Penn invests, *Cash*, $500; *Real Estate*, $5000.

2.—Sold N. Frederick, on %, 2 doz. Gent's Silk Handkerchiefs, 24, @ 40¢; 6 pcs. Amoskeag Sheeting, 130 yds., @ 10¢; 4 do. Mixed Cassimeres, 100 yds., @ 50¢ - - - - - Rec'd Cash of Henry Fish, in full of %, $500 - - - - - Paid Cash for Stationery and Printing, $30.

3.—Sold Ira Packard on his acceptance, at 10 days, 1 case Child's Metallic Tip Shoes, 60 prs., @ 50¢; 2 do. Child's Heel Gaiters, 96 prs., @ 63¢; 3 pcs. English Tweed, 27 yds., @ $1.

4.—Sold Wm. T. Bush, on %, 4 cases Men's Congress Gaiters, 96 prs., @ $1.50; 2 do. Gent's Canada Ties, 24 prs., @ $1.75 - - - - - Sold James Magoon, for Cash, 1 piece Striped Velvet, 10 yds., @ $5; 6 do. Paper Cambrics, 72 yds., @ 8¢; 10 do. Lynn Cottons, 300 yds., at 11¢.

5.—Paid Cash for petty Expenses, $3.75 - - - - - Sold Robert Smith, on his note at 60 days, 3 pcs. Lancaster Gingham, 125 yds., @ 10¢; 6 do. Scotch Plaid, 240 yds., @ 13¢ - - - - - Bought of Star, Barnum & Seeley, Invoice of Merchandise, amounting to $5000; paid Cash, $2500; Note, at 6 months, $2500.

6.—Rec'd Cash on % of David Coleman, $500 - - - - - Sold Roger Williams, for Cash, 1 case Misses Cork Sole Shoes, 60 prs., @ 75¢; 1 do. Gent's Paris Gaiters, 24 prs., @ $1.75 - - - - - Rec'd Cash for petty Sales, $25.50.

7.—Sold John Fitch, on %, 3 doz. Elastic Hoop Skirts, 36, @ $2.50; 1 doz. "Empress" do., 12, @ $2; 3 pcs. Check Marseilles, 30 yds., @ 50¢ - - - - - Sold Samuel Nash, for Cash, 3 pcs. English Tweed, 27 yds., @ $1; 5 do. Corduroy, 250 yds., @ 75¢ - - - - - Rec'd Cash of Wm. T. Bush, on %, $50.

9.—Paid John R. Penn, Cash on private %, $100 - - - - - Paid Cash for petty Expenses, $7.50.

69

10.—Sold John Anderson, for Cash, 3 cases Ladies' Extra Balmoral Boots, 144 prs., at $2; 2 cases Ladies' "Opera" Gaiters, 48, @ $1.75.

12.—Paid S. S. Packard, Cash on private %, $75 - - - - - Sold Thos. Hunter, on %, 6 pcs. Merrimack Prints, 210 yds., @ 9¢; 5 do. "Union" Prints, 150 yds., @ 8¢; 7 do. Lancaster Prints, 244 yds., @ 8½¢; 4 do. Orange Prints, 120 yds., @ 8½¢ - - - - - Rec'd Cash for petty Sales, $10.38.

13.—Rec'd Cash of David Coleman, in full of %, $400 - - - - - Sold John Howard, on %, 3 pcs. Lancaster Gingham, 125 yds., @ 10¢; 2 do. French Merino, 40 yds., @ 50¢; 5 do. Bar. Muslin, 90 yds., @ 14¢.

14.—Sold Robert Coons, for Cash, 6 pcs. Fancy Linens, 36 yds., @ $2; 5 do. English Prints, 200 yds., @ 20¢; 6 do. Parametta (Maroon), 300 yds., @ 75¢ - - - - - Paid Cash for Repairing Store, $75.

16.—Rec'd Cash of John Fitch, in full of %, $129 - - - - - - Sold Henry Fish, on %, 5 pcs. Amoskeag Stripes, 120 yds., @ 12½¢; 4 do. Pepperell Sheeting, 160 yds., @ 10¢; 4 do. Auburn Sheeting, 120 yds., @ 15¢.

17.—Rec'd Cash in full of Robert Fulton's %, $750 - - - - - - Sold Simon Walker, on his note at 60 days, 4 cases Men's Thick Boots, 48 prs., @ $1.25; 2 do. Double-Soled Boots, 24 prs., @ $1.50.

20.—Sold Geo. F. Smith, for Cash, 2 cases Women's Walking Shoes, 120 prs., @ 50¢; 2 do. Jenny Lind Gaiters, 24 prs., @ $1.15; 2 do. "Opera" Gaiters, 24 prs., @ $1.75 - - - - - - Paid Clerk hire in Cash, $65.

21.—Rec'd Cash of Henry Fish, in full of %, $49.

STATEMENT OF RESULTS.

The general results of the above transactions properly recorded are shown in the following schedule. The statement to be rendered by the student should be more in detail, taking as an example the statement on page 67.

Resources.			Liabilities.		
Personal Accounts	315	54	Notes, payable	2500	
Notes, receivable	1457	18	S. S. P.'s Net Investment . .	9025	
Cash	5286	49	J. R. P.'s	5400	
Merchandise (per Inv.) . . .	4500				
Real Estate	5000				
NET LOSS.	365	79			
	16925			16925	

Set 4.—Single Entry.

FURNITURE AND CABINET BUSINESS.

(TWO PARTNERS, ADMITTING A THIRD.)

DAY-BOOK, SALES-BOOK, LEDGER, CASH-BOOK, AND TIME-BOOK.

USING THE SALES-BOOK AS PRINCIPAL BOOK, AND GIVING INSTRUCTIONS AS TO A CHANGE IN BUSINESS.

Prosperous.

REMARKS.

The capabilities of Single Entry Book-keeping are fairly presented in this set, and it will be found that this form of record has much in it worthy of consideration. At the best, however, Single Entry is an incomplete system, and has no advantages over Double Entry; while, on the other hand, Double Entry, retaining all that is vital in Single Entry, supplements its best achievements by such results, tests, and statistical facts as are essential to a complete knowledge of business operations.

However, as Single Entry Book-keeping is in vogue, and as it will continue to be, even in some of the most reputable houses, it behooves the accountant to become conversant with its characteristics and its possibilities.

The materials from which the transactions in this set are constructed, were obtained from an extensive cabinet warehouse in New York, and the routine has the merit, at least, of being business-like. The forms of the books, and arrangement of the various records, are submitted as the most simple and practical in use.

One important feature in the set is the use of the Sales-Book distinct from the Day-Book. In Set III., although a Sales-Book is used, all sales *on credit* are first transferred to the Day-Book, and from thence posted into the Ledger. Here, however, the credit sales are posted to the personal accounts *directly from the Sales Book*. This affords a great saving of time, and is, in all respects, quite as satisfactory. The figures in the margin of the Sales-Book refer to the Ledger page to which the amounts are posted; the initials " C. B." and " B. B." indicate that the result of the sales thus marked, are shown in the Cash Book and Bill Book. The former of these is exhibited at length; the latter has been omitted, although it is expected that the learner will supply it, after the form given in Set III.

The taking in of a new partner forms another important feature of the set, and one which will afford the learner some of the most valuable hints connected with Accounts. It is a settled principle in Book-keeping, or should be, that whenever any change in the business occurs, the existing resources and liabilities of the concern should be made apparent; and, consequently, the proprietors' accounts should represent their net investment *at the time of the change.* The same rule holds good respecting the landmarks of business, or the financial eras, such as the close of a fiscal year, or any important event which makes it necessary to exhibit on the main books the exact condition of the business.

In the case under consideration, the existing partners, "Lester & Brown," propose to admit a new partner, who shall invest equally with them, and share equally in the gains and losses. The partners' accounts now show only their *original* investment; and it will be evident that, if the new partner invests an equal amount, he will unjustly become a joint-partner in the gains which have already accrued, but which remain unacknowledged in the business. The original partners, it is plain, are entitled to all the avails of the business previous to admitting the new partner, and if their own proper accounts do not show what this net amount is, they should be made to. Therefore, before deciding how much the new partner should invest to place him on an equal footing with his associates, it becomes necessary to credit the original partners with their respective gains. With this view the statement on the third page of the Day-Book is made, and the partners thereafter credited, each with his net gain. The partners' accounts in the Ledger are then closed up, and the balances brought down as a new capital, which is an indication of the amount that the new partner must invest.

The general statement which follows this set affords, perhaps, as convenient a form for such statements as any in use. The student cannot too carefully study the philosophy of these, nor be too particular in drawing them up, as to their neatness and perspicuity. An obscure or insufficient statement of a business, however prosperous and satisfactory may be the condition which it aims to show, is like a good story so bunglingly told that its chief points are obscure, and its moral entirely lost sight of.

Brooklyn, April 1, 1879.

James Lester and Robert Brown enter into Copartnership this day, as Dealers in Furniture and Cabinet-ware, under the firm-title of "Lester & Brown;" Mr. Lester transferring to the firm the assets and liabilities of a former business, and Mr. Brown investing an equivalent in cash, as per terms of contract.

(1	James Lester,	Cr.			
	By Investment, as follows:				
	Mdse. (finished articles), per I. B.,	$3000 00			
	Materials and Unfinished work,,	2500 00			
	Tools and Implements,	300 00			
	Notes on hand, per Bill Book,	1375 00			
	Balance of David Owens' %,	230 00			
	" " Thomas Webster's %,	57 30			
	" " Timothy Paywell's %,	175 00	7637	30

(1	James Lester,	Dr.			
	To the following debts, assumed by firm:				
	Note favor Joseph Wiggins, due Ap. 20,	$500 00			
	" " Peter Jones, " Sep. 10,	250 00			
	Balance due Austin Packard on %,	175 00			
	" " I. W. Bulkley, "	230 00	1155	

(2	Robert Brown,	Cr.		
	By Cash,		6482	30

(3	David Owens,	Dr.	
	To balance due I. L.,		230

(4	Thomas Webster,	Dr.		
	To balance due I. L.,		57	30

Brooklyn, April 1, 1879.

(5)	Timothy Taywell,	Dr.		
	To balance due J. L.,		175	
	"			
(6)	Austin Packard,	Cr.		
	By balance due from J. L.,		175	
	"			
(7)	J. W. Bulkley,	Cr.		
	By balance due from J. L.,		230	
	2			
(3)	David Owens,	Cr.		
	By Cash to bal. %,		230	
	4			
(9)	H. W. Clark,	Cr.		
	By Cash on %,		50	
	15			
(4)	Thomas Webster,	Cr.		
	By Cash in full of %,		57	30
	18			
(6)	Austin Packard,	Dr.		
	To Cash in full of %,		175	
	20			
(10)	Richard Bannister,	Cr.		
	By Cash on %,		30	
	25			
(11)	Roger Bacon,	Cr.		
	By Cash in full of %,		43	50

Brooklyn, April 27, 1879.

Richard Bannister; Cr.		37
By Note @ 30 ds., to Balance %,		

———— NEW FIRM. ————

———— May 1 ————

Messrs. Lester & Brown have this day associated with them, Robert Lincoln, who is to invest an equal amount of capital, and share equally in gains and losses, as per contract. The books of "Lester & Brown" are therefore made to exhibit their resources and liabilities, each partner being credited with his share of the net gain, and the balances brought down as a new investment. The new firm is to be styled "Lester, Brown & Co."

Following is an exhibit of Lester & Brown's affairs:

———— Resources. ————

Bal. due on personal acc'ts, per Ledger,	$416 00		
Cash on hand, per Cash Book,	5874 38		
Notes '' '' Bill Book,	1016 50		
Value of Finished Stock, per inven'y,	4250 00		
'' Unfinished '' '' ''	1875 00		
'' Tools and Implements,	500 00	13931	88

———— Liabilities. ————

Bal. due on personal acc'ts, per Ledger,	175 00		
Peter Jones' note,	250 00	425	
Present Worth,		13506	88
James Lester's investment,	6482 30		
Robert Brown's ''	6482 30	12964	60
Net Gain,		542	28
James Lester's ½ net gain, $271 14			
Robert Brown's ½ '' '' 271 14	542 28		

Brooklyn, May 1, 1879.

(1)	James Lester,	Cr.		
	By Net gain, per statement,		271	14
(2)	Robert Brown,	Cr.		
	By Net gain, per statement,		271	14
(14)	Robert Lincoln,	Cr.		
	By Cash invested,		6753	44
(15)	Central Bank,	Dr.		
	To Cash deposited,		12000	
	5			
(12)	John Anderson,	Cr.		
	By Cash in full of %,		65	
	8			
(5)	Timothy Paywell,	Cr.		
	By Cash in full of %,		175	
	9			
(7)	J. W. Bulkley,	Dr.		
	To Cash in full of %,		121	
	31			
(1)	James Lester,	Cr.		
	By Net gain, per statement,		187	73
(2)	Robert Brown,	Cr.		
	By Net gain, per statement,		187	73
(14)	Robert Lincoln,	Cr.		
	By Net gain, per statement,		187	74

1

Brooklyn, April 2, 1879.

8	A. A. Low, *Brooklyn,*	
	1 Rosewood Tete-a-tete,	$60 00
	1 Gothic Mahogany Bedstead,	20 00
	6 Mahogany Chairs, Carved,	25 00
	1 Marble-top Table,	15 00	120
	Chgd. to %.	

"

C.B.	H. W. Beecher, *Brooklyn,*	
	1 Dressing Bureau, Serpentine front,	$22 00
	1 Lounge for study,	15 00
	1 Gothic Hall Stand, R. W.,	24 00	61
	Recd. Cash.	

3

9	H. W. Clark, *Williamsburg,*	
	6 Cane-bottom Chairs, Mgy.,	$15 00
	1 Black Walnut Tete-a-tete,	25 00
	1 Mgy. Centre Table,	14 00
	1 " Card Table, O. G. front,	7 00	61
	Chgd. to %.	

4

B.B.	J. J. Powell, *Jamaica,*	
	1 Card Table, Mgy.,	$8 00
	1 Sofa " B. W.,	9 00
	1 Piano Stool, R. W.,	7 50
	2 Small Wash Stands, @ $2 50,	5 00	29 50
	Note @ 30 ds.	

"

C.B.	Thomas Proctor, *Yonkers.*	
	1 French Bedstead, B. W.,	15
	Recd. Cash.	

78

7	J. W. Bulkley,	Williamsburg,	
	1 pair Ottomans, B. W.,	$10 00	
	1 Lounge, Brocatelle,	15 00	
	6 Parlor Chairs, R. W.,	30 00	55
		Chgd. to %.	
	6		
C.B.	John N. Pattison,	New York,	
	1 Piano Stool,	$8 00	
	1 Music Rack,	4 00	12
		Recd. Cash.	
	7		
10	Richard Bannister,	Chester,	
	1 Stuffed-back Chair,	$15 00	
	1 Cottage Bedstead, B. W.,	12 00	
	1 Gothic ,,	20 00	
	4 Parlor Chairs, Mgy.,	16 00	
	1 Corner Stand, ,,	4 00	67
		Chgd. to %.	
	,,		
C.B.	Henry W. Taylor,	Brooklyn,	
	1 Double-leaf Secretary,	$35 00	
	1 Enameled cloth Lounge,	10 00	45
		Recd. Cash.	
	8		
C.B.	T. L. Cuyler,	Brooklyn,	
	1 Extension Dining Table,	$14 00	
	6 Kitchen Chairs,	3 00	
	1 Book Case, R. W.,	40 00	
	1 Hall Stand, ,,	15 00	72
		Recd. Cash.	

3

Brooklyn, April 10, 1879.

C.B.	Robert McGrath,	Islip,		
	2 Quartette Tables, Mgy.,		$5 00	
	1 Sofa Table, Lyre front,		11 00	
	1 Large Arm Chair,		12 00	
	2 Sew. Chairs, Cane bot.,		6 50	34 50
		Recd. Cash.		

13

C.B.	James Smith,	Hempstead,		
	12 Dining Chairs, @ $1 50		$18 00	
	1 " Table,		15 00	33
		Recd. Cash.		

15

11	Roger Bacon,	Haverstraw,		
	1 Lady's Arm Chair, R. W.,		$10 00	
	1 " Sewing " "		7 50	
	1 Card Table, "		6 00	
	1 Cabinet Box, R. W.,		20 00	43 50
		Chgd. to %.		

18

C.B.	William F. Turner,	Brooklyn,		
	1 Single Bedstead,		$6 00	
	6 Cottage Chairs, @ $1 75		10 50	
	1 Quartette Table,		5 00	21 50
		Recd. Cash.		

20

12	John J. Anderson,	Brooklyn,		
	1 set Enam. Furniture,			65
		Chgd. to %.		

25

B.B.	James E. Jenkins,	Brooklyn,		
	1 Sofa Bedstead, Patent,		$45 00	
	6 Parlor Chairs, Broc.,		30 00	75
		Note @ 60 ds.		

Brooklyn, April 28, 1879. **4**

C.B.	David Woods,	Red Hook,	
	1 Tete-a-tete, B. W. and Broc.,	$40 00	
	1 Easy Rocker, ,, ,, ,,	25 00	
	1 Corner Stand,	4 00	69
		Recd. Cash.	

—————— 30 ——————

9	H. W. Clark,	Williamsburg,	
	1 Sofa Bedstead, Patent,		45
		Chgd. to %.	

——————— NEW FIRM. ———————

—————— May 1 ——————

C.B.	Peter Jamieson,	Morrisania,	
	1 "Sleepy Hollow" Chair,	$18 00	
	1 Enameled Bedstead,	20 00	
	1 ,, Wash Stand,	5 00	43
		Recd. Cash.	

—————— 3 ——————

8	A. A. Low,	Brooklyn,	
	2 Gothic Chairs, B. W. stuffed,	$30 00	
	1 set Enam. Furniture,	75 00	105
		Chgd. to %.	

—————— 5 ——————

13	Joseph Brooks,	Bellvale.	
	2 Cupboard Washstands, @ $6 00	$12 00	
	1 Hat Rack,	5 00	
	1 Dining Table,	14 00	
	1 Black Walnut Crib,	5 00	36
		Chgd. to %.	

5

Brooklyn, May 6, 1879.

7	*J. W. Bulkley,* *Williamsburg,*		
	1 Centre Table, B. W., Carved,	$25 00	
	1 Bureau, Serpentine Front,	24 50	
	1 Side "What-not,"	4 50	54
	Chgd. to %.		

10

10	*Richard Bannister,* *Chester,*		
	1 Reclining Chair, Patent,	$12 50	
	1 High Book Case, B. W.,	40 00	
	1 pair Footstools,	4 50	57
	Chgd. to %.		

15

C. B.	*C. L. Derby,* *New York,*		
	1 set Enameled Furniture,	$75 00	
	1 Tete-a-tete,	30 00	
	1 Rosewood Sofa,	60 00	165
	Recd. Cash.		

18

C. B.	*Ivison, Phinney & Co.,* *New York,*		
	1 B. W. Lib'y Book Case,		75
	Recd. Cash.		

20

C. B.	*W. L. Stimson,* *Penn Yan.*		
	2 plain Wash Stands,	$4 00	
	1 French Bedstead, B. W.,	25 00	
	1 Single " "	10 00	
	6 Dining Chairs, @ $1 50,	9 00	
	3 Parlor " " 4 50,	13 50	61 50
	Recd. Cash.		

Brooklyn, May 20, 1879.

16	Str. Isaac Newton,	North River,			
	6 Rosewood Tete-a-tetes,	@ $35 00	$210 00		
	24 ,, Chairs,	,, 5 00	120 00		
	3 Stuffd. Broc. Arm Chairs,	,, 25 00	75 00		
	1 Carved Rosewood Centre Table,		50 00	455	
	Chgd. to %.				

25

8	A. A. Low,	Brooklyn,			
	150 Orchestra Chairs, for Academy of				
	Music, @ $4 00,			600	
	Chgd. to %.				

28

C. B.	George McDougal,	New York,			
	1 Hall Stand,		$4 00		
	6 Parlor Chairs, @ $2 75,		16 50		
	1 Wash Stand,		10 00	30	50
	Recd. Cash.				

30

C. B.	Abraham Fuller,	Jamaica,			
	1 Black Walnut Sofa,		$30 00		
	1 Tete-a-tete,		25 00		
	1 Large Dining Table,		16 00		
	2 Gothic Chairs,		10 00	81	
	Recd. Cash.				

,,

C. B.	R. Van Norman,,	New York,			
	1 Piano Stool,		$10 00		
	1 Music Rack,		5 00		
	2 Arm-chairs, Rosewood,		45 00	60	
	Recd. Cash.				

1
Dr. James Lester. **Cr.**

1879						1879					
Apr.	1	Sund. debts,	1	1155		Apr.	1	By invest't,	1	7637	30
May	1	To balance,		6753	44	May	1	,, Net gain,	4	271	14
				7908	44					7908	44
May	31	To balance,		6941	17	May	1	By balance,		6753	44
						,,	31	,, Net gain,		187	73
				6941	17					6941	17
						June	1	By balance,		6941	17

2
Dr. Robert Brown. **Cr.**

1879						1879					
May	1	To balance,		6753	44	Apr.	1	By Cash inv.,	1	6482	30
						May	1	,, Net gain,	4	271	14
				6753	44					6753	44
May	31	To balance,		6941	17	May	1	By balance,		6753	44
						,,	31	,, Net gain,		187	73
				6941	17					6941	17
						June	1	By balance,		6941	17

3
Dr. David Owens. **Cr.**

1879						1879					
Apr.	1	Bal. due I. L.	1	230		Apr.	2	By Cash,	2	230	

4
Dr. Thomas Webster. **Cr.**

1879						1879					
Apr.	1	Bal. due I. L.	1	57	30	Apr.	15	By Cash,	2	57	30

5

Dr.   Timothy Paywell.   Cr.

1879					1879				
Apr.	1	Bal. due S. L.	2	175	May	8	By Cash,	4	175

6

Dr.   Austin Packard.   Cr.

1879					1879				
Apr.	18	By Cash,	2	175	Apr.	1	Bal. from S. L.	1	175

7

Dr.   J. W. Bulkley.   Cr.

1879					1879				
Apr.	5	To sund. S. B.	2	55	Apr.	1	Bal. from S. L.	1	230
,,	30	Balance,		175					
				230					230
May	6	To sund. S. B.	5	54	May	1	By balance,		175
,,	9	Cash,	4	121					
				175					175

8

Dr.   A. A. Low.   Cr.

1879					1879				
Apr.	2	To sund. S. B.	1	120	May	31	By balance,		825
May	3	,, ,, ,,	4	105					
,,	25	150 Chairs ,,	6	600					
				825					
May	31	To balance,		825					

9

Dr.   H. W. Clark.   Cr.

1879						1879					
Apr.	3	To sund. S. B.	1	61		Apr.	4	By Cash,	2	50	
,,	30	,, ,,	4	45		,,	30	Balance,		56	
				106						106	
May	1	To balance,		56							

10

Dr.   Richard Bannister.   Cr.

1879						1879					
Apr.	7	To sund. S. B.	2	67		Apr.	20	By Cash,	2	30	
						,,	27	Note,	3	37	
				67						67	
May	10	To sund. S. B.	5	57							

11

Dr.   Roger Bacon.   Cr.

1879						1879					
Apr.	15	To sund. S. B.	3	43	50	Apr.	25	By Cash,	2	43	50

12

Dr.   John J. Anderson.   Cr.

1879						1879				
Apr.	20	To sund. S. B.	3	65		May	5	By Cash,	4	65

13

Dr.   Joseph Brooks.   Cr.

1879								
May	5	To sund. S. B.	4	36				

14

Dr.   Robert Lincoln.   Cr.

1879						1879						
May	31	To balance,		6941	18	May	1	By Invest't,	4	6753	44
						,,	31	,, Net gain,	,,	187	74
				6941	18					6941	18
						June	1	By balance,		6941	18

15

Dr.   Central Bank.   Cr.

1879								
May	1	Cash dep.,	4	12000				

16

Dr.   Steamer Isaac Newton.   Cr.

1879								
May	20	To sund. S. B.	6	455				

_____ Cash. _____   Received.

1879						
Apr.	1	Am't invested, Robert Brown,			6482	30
	2	Rec'd of H. W. Beecher, per S. B.,	61			
	,,	David Owens, in full of %,	230			
	4	Thomas Proctor, per S. B.,	15			
	,,	H. W. Clark, on %,	50			
	6	John N. Pattison, per S. B.,	12			
	7	Henry W. Taylor, ,, ,,	45			
	,,	Am't due on John Simpson's note,	500			
	8	T. L. Cuyler, per S. B.	72			
	10	Robert McGrath,	34	50		
	12	James Smith,	33			
	15	Thomas Webster, in full of %,	57	30		
	18	William Turner, per S. B.,	21	50		
	20	Richard Bannister, on %,	30			
	25	Roger Bacon, in full of %,	43	50		
	28	David Woods, per S. B.,	69		1273	80
					7756	10
		Balance brought down,			5874	38
May	1	Am't invested by Robert Lincoln,	6753	44		
	,,	Rec'd of Peter Jamieson, per S. B.,	43			
	5	John Anderson, in full of %,	65			
	8	Timothy Paywell, ,, ,,	175			
	15	C. L. Derby, per S. B.,	165			
	18	Ivison, Phinney & Co., S. B.,	75			
	20	W. L. Stimson, ,,	61	50		
	28	George McDougal, ,,	30	50		
	30	Abraham Fuller, ,,	81			
	,,	B. Van Norman, ,,	60		7509	44
					13383	82
		Balance brought down,			503	02

_____ Cash. _____   Paid out

1879							
Apr.	1	Paid for stat'y, $5; Post. stamps, $3,	8			
	2	J. Stevens & Co. bill Box Lumber,	75			
	,,	for Glue and Varnish p. Exp. Book,	18	75		
	4	,, Hair Cloth, per J. White's Bill,	150			
	5	,, Copy. Press, $6; Let. Book, $2,	8			
	6	Workmen wages to date, p. Time B.,	128	17		
	8	Simpson's bill for B. W. Lumber,	350			
	10	Petty expenses, per Expense Book,	15	30		
	13	Workmen's wages, per Time Book,	121	33		
	15	Insurance on building & contents,	85			
	18	Austin Packard, in full of %,	175			
	20	Workmen's wages, per Time Book,	113	17		
	,,	J. Wiggin's note,	500			
	25	Drayage, $10; Post. stamps, $3,	13			
	27	Workmen's wages, per Time Book,	121		1881	72
		Balance on hand,			5874	38
					7756	10
May	1	Deposited in Central Bank,	12000			
	3	Paid Sundry expenses, per Expen. Book,	18	75		
	4	Fisher & Bird's bill for Marble,	115			
	,,	Workmen's wages, per Time Book,	117	50		
	9	J. W. Bulkley, in full of %,	121			
	11	Workmen's wages, per Time Book,	128	75		
	15	Sundry expenses, per Expen. Book,	24	30		
	18	Workmen's wages, per Time Book,	98	50		
	20	L. Johnson's bill for Plush, etc.,	124			
	25	Workmen's wages, per Time Book,	113	75		
	28	Sundry expenses, per Expen. Book,	19	25	12880	50
		Balance on hand,			503	02
					13383	52

TIME BOOK.

NAMES.	APRIL, 1879. Wages per Week.	1 M	2 T	3 W	4 Th	5 F	6 S	Amt.	8 M	9 T	10 W	11 Th	12 F	13 S	Amt.	15 M	16 T	17 W	18 Th	19 F	20 S	Amt.	22 M	23 T	24 W	25 Th	26 F	27 S	Amt.
Robert Wood	20	√	√	√	√	√	√	√20 50	√	√	√	√	√	√	√20	√	√	√	√	√	√	√20	√	√	√	√	√	√	√20 33
Samuel Burns	15	√	√	√	√	√	√	√12 67	√	√	√	√	√	√	√15	√	√	√	√	√	√	√15	√	√	√	√	√	√	√15 67
P. O'Toole	10	√	√	√	√	√	√	√6														√10							
James Murphy	10	√	√	√	√	√	√	√10	√	√	√	√	√	√	√10	√	√	√	√	√	√	√10	√	√	√	√	√	√	√3
Pat. McGann	10	√	√	√	√	√	√	√10 33	√	√	√	√	√	√	√10	√	√	√	√	√	√	√6	√	√	√	√	√	√	√6
John Turk	6	√	√	√	√	√	√	√3	√	√	√	√	√	√	√6	√	√	√	√	√	√	√6	√	√	√	√	√	√	√6
Peter Winns	6	√	√	√	√	√	√	√6	√	√	√	√	√	√	√6	√	√	√	√	√	√	√4	√	√	√	√	√	√	√6
Abel Jones	6	√	√	√	√	√	√	√6	√	√	√	√	√	√	√2	√	√	√	√	√	√	√4	√	√	√	√	√	√	√6
A. Jackson	6	√	√	√	√	√	√	√5	√	√	√	√	√	√	√4	√	√	√	√	√	√	√6	√	√	√	√	√	√	√6
R. Porter	6	√	√	√	√	√	√	√5	√	√	√	√	√	√	√4	√	√	√	√	√	√	√6	√	√	√	√	√	√	√6
P. Sanford	6	√	√	√	√	√	√	√5	√	√	√	√	√	√	√4	√	√	√	√	√	√	√6	√	√	√	√	√	√	√6
F. Molloy	6	√	√	√	√	√	√	√5	√	√	√	√	√	√	√6	√	√	√	√	√	√	√6	√	√	√	√	√	√	√6
H. Wait	6	√	√	√	√	√	√	√6	√	√	√	√	√	√	√6	√	√	√	√	√	√	√6	√	√	√	√	√	√	√6
Henry Trim	6	√	√	√	√	√	√	√6	√	√	√	√	√	√	√3	√	√	√	√	√	√	√4 17	√	√	√	√	√	√	√6
P. Bush	5	√	√	√	√	√	√	√5	√	√	√	√	√	√	√5	√	√	√	√	√	√	√5	√	√	√	√	√	√	√5
A. Burr	5	√	√	√	√	√	√	√5	√	√	√	√	√	√	√5	√	√	√	√	√	√	√5	√	√	√	√	√	√	√5
Thos. Park	5	√	√	√	√	√	√	√5 67	√	√	√	√	√	√	√5	√	√	√	√	√	√	√5	√	√	√	√	√	√	√5
R. Mann	5	√	√	√	√	√	√	√1	√	√	√	√	√	√	√5	√	√	√	√	√	√	√5	√	√	√	√	√	√	√5
H. Poore	5	√	√	√	√	√	√	√5	√	√	√	√	√	√	√5	√	√	√	√	√	√	√5	√	√	√	√	√	√	√5
S. Parker	3	√	√	√	√	√	√	√3	√	√	√	√	√	√	√3	√	√	√	√	√	√	√1	√	√	√	√	√	√	√3
Total.								128 17							121 33							118 17							121

90

STATEMENT

THE following Statement is in most respects like those which have preceded it; the only difference being in the form of expressing the gains. The gains are obtained in the usual way, but the statement gives the *proof* in the form of addition, rather than the process by subtraction. The sum of these amounts, or the total present worth, must, of course, equal the sum of the resources.

_____ Resources. _____					
1. *From Ledger Accounts.*—Balances due:					
A. A. Low, - - - - - - - - - - -	825				
H. W. Clark, - - - - - - - - - - -	56				
R. Bannister, - - - - - - - - - - -	57				
Joseph Brooks, - - - - - - - - -	36				
Central Bank, - - - - - - - - - -	12000				
Steamer Isaac Newton, - - - - - - -	455				
2. *From Cash Book.*—Balance of Cash on hand, - -	503	02			
3. *From Bill Book.*—Notes on hand, - - - - -	1016	50			
4. *From Inventory.*—Valuation of Property,					
Finished Stock on hand, - - - - - - - -	4750				
Unfinished, - - - - - - - - - - - -	875				
Tools and Implements, - - - - - - -	500			21073	52
_____ Liabilities. _____					
P. Jones' note, - - - - - - - - - - - -	250				
James Lester's Investment, - - - -	$6753	44			
" " ⅓ Net Gain, - - - - -	187	73			
" " *Present Worth,* - - -			6941	17		
Robert Brown's Investment, - - - -	$6753	44			
" " ⅓ Net Gain, - - - - -	187	73			
" " *Present Worth,* - - -			6941	17		
Robert Lincoln's Investment, - - - -	$6753	44			
" " ⅓ Net gain, - - - - -	187	74			
" " *Present Worth,* - - -			6941	18		
				21073	52

EXAMPLES FOR PRACTICE.

EXAMPLE I.—A. and B. are equal partners, investing each $10000. At the end of a year they desire to take C. into co-partnership upon condition that he will invest equally with them, and share equally in the results of the business. The following is a statement of their affairs previous to uniting with C.:

Personal Accounts: John Jones, Dr. $1500, Cr. $700 ; Robert Fulton, Dr. $5000; James Webb, Dr. $1750, Cr. $1000 ; Clarence Shook, Dr. $5000, Cr. $2500 ; Lewis Lyman, Cr. $4000, Dr. $3000 ; W. F. Norman, Cr. $2000, Dr. $1500 ; Merchandise unsold, $7500 ; Notes on hand, $6000 ; Notes outstanding, $2500; Cash on hand, $2000.

Required a statement showing the gain or loss during business, and the net capital of each partner at closing.

EXAMPLE II.—C. and D. enter into co-partnership, C. to furnish the capital, and D. to devote his time to the business—gains and losses to be divided equally. C. invests $10000, and during the year withdraws $2000. D. withdraws $1500. At the close of the year, they have: Cash, $3000 ; Personal accounts, $1500 ; Merchandise, $10000 ; Notes, $1750 ; they owe, on notes and personal accounts, $5000.

What is the gain or loss in business? What is each partner's capital at closing?

EXAMPLE III.—J. and K. enter into co-partnership for the purpose of conducting a Building business ; each to receive interest at 7% on his net investment, and the gain or loss to be divided equally. J. invests: Materials and Implements, $5000 ; Unfinished contracts, $6750 ; Notes, $4800 ; Personal accounts, $10000; and the firm assume to pay for him a liability of $1000. K. invests: Cash, $10000 ; Notes, $15000. At the close of the year their books show the following condition: Cash on hand, $15000; Notes, $5700 ; Interest on same, $500; Materials and Implements, $18000 ; Personal accounts, $9400.

What is the net gain or loss? What is each partner's capital at closing?

EXAMPLE IV.—The following statement exhibits the condition of Horton & Randall's business at the end of the year:

Resources: Mdse., $7500 ; Cash, $4375. *Personal Accounts, viz.:* H. M. Monsanto, $575 ; F. M. Choquill, $170 : C. E. Carhart, $325. Liabilities: To D. B. Ivison on %, $1750 ; To D. W. Fish, on their note, $1000. The original investments were : B. Horton, Cash, $5000 ; A. W. Randall, Cash, $3000; Mdse., $2000. Mr. Horton has drawn out for private use $1275 ; Mr. Randall, do., $1450.

Required, the gain or loss of the business, and the condition of each partner's account after the net results have been equally divided.

PRACTICAL EXERCISES.

[To be written up after the manner of Set 4.]

TRANSACTIONS.—FOURTH SERIES.

June 1.—William Jones and Thomas Mason, enter into copartnership. WILLIAM JONES *invests :* Mdse., $4750 ; Tools and Implements, $750 ; John Jacobs' note, dated May 4 @ 30 ds., for $500, and Wm. Carter's of Apr. 19, @ 2 mos., for $1000 ; Peter Filkin's %, $500 ; Robert Hall's do., $700 - - - - - THOMAS MASON *invests :* Cash, $8200 - - - - - Sold W. D. Packard, on %, 1 set Enameled Furniture, $75 ; 2 Hair Mattresses, @ $12 each ; 1 Mahogany Arm Chair, $15.

2.—Paid Cash for Stationery, $20 - - - - - Sold Robert Banks, for Cash, 1 doz. Dining Chairs, $20 ; 1 Hall Stand, $8 ; 1 Mahogany Bedstead, $12 - - - - - Paid Cash for Lumber, $25 - - - - - Sold George Chrysler, on his note @ 30 ds., 1 Child's Crib, B.W., $6 ; 1 Mahogany Bureau, $25 ; 1 Tete-a-tete, R. W., $30.

3.—Received Cash of Robert Hall, on %, $300 - - - - - Sold George A. Crocker, on %, 1 Hall Stand, $6 ; 2 Light Washstands, 1 @ $5, and 1 @ $7 ; 12 Kitchen Chairs, @ 75¢ - - - - - Sold John Hall, for Cash, 1 French Bedstead, $15.

5.—Paid Workmen, Cash to date, $165 - - - - - Sold A. W. Betts, on %, 10 Cane Bottom Chairs, @ $1.75 each ; 1 Black Walnut Tete-a-tete, $30 ; 1 Card Table, $10 ; 3 small Washstands, @ $2.50 each - - - - - Sold James Morgan, for Cash, 1 Black Walnut Book-case, $40 ; 1 Double-leaf Secretary, $30.

6.—Received Cash for John Jacobs' note, due this day, $500 - - - - - Sold Charles Williams, on his note @ 60 ds., 1 pair Ottomans, $12 ; 1 Piano Stool, $7 ; 8 Brocatelle Parlor Chairs, @ $4 each ; 1 Sofa Table, $15 - - - - - Bo't of Clark Dunham, on %, 1 lot Black Walnut Lumber, $900.

7.—Sold A. W. Betts, on %, 1 Mahogany Centre Table, $15 ; 1 Cottage Bedstead, $10 ; 1 Corner Stand, $5 - - - - - Sold James W. Lusk, for Cash, 1 Black Walnut Book-case, $50 - - - - - Received Cash in full of Peter Filkin's %, $500.

8.—Sold J. C. Buttre, for Cash, 1 Dressing Bureau (serpentine front), $25 ; 1 Study Lounge, $12 ; 1 Extension Dining Table, $17 - - - - - Sold Wm. T. Brooks, on %, 1 Rosewood Tete-a-tete, $50.

9.—Sold James Moore, for Cash, 1 Quartette Table, $6 ; 6 Parlor Chairs, @ $5 each ; 1 set Enameled Furniture, $50.

10.—Paid Cash for Gas Bill, $14.30 - - - - - Received Cash of A. W. Betts, in full of %, $_____.

12.—Paid Workmen, Cash to date, $275 - - - - - Sold Geo. A. Crocker, on %, 6 Parlor Chairs, @ $3 ; 12 Dining do., @ $1.50 ; 1 Clock, $5.

13.—Sold Benj. F. Butler, on %, 8 doz. Camp Stools, 96 @ 50¢ each ; 1 Portable Secretary, $25 - - - - - Received Cash on %, of W. D. Packard, $75.

15.—Sold Robert Hall, on %, 6 Gothic Chairs @ $5 each ; 1 French Bedstead, $15 ; 2 Washstands, @ $4 each ; - - - - Sold W. J. Curtiss, for Cash, 1 Book-case, $40 ; 4 Library Chairs, @ $7 each ; 1 large Rocking Chair, $15.

17.—Paid Workmen, Cash to date, $218 - - - - - Received Cash of Geo. A. Crocker, in full of %, $———— - - - - - Sold J. C. Banks, for Cash, 1 Double Bedstead, $10 ; 1 Single do., $9.

18.—Paid Clark Dunham, Cash on %, $500 - - - - - Sold John Banks, on his note @ 30 ds., 1 Bureau, $30 ; 1 Sofa Bedstead, $45.

19.—Sold W. D. Packard, on %, 12 Kitchen Chairs, @ $1 each ; 3 Common Bedsteads, @ $5 each ; 1 Office Desk, $15 - - - - - Sold W. T. Brooks, on %, 1 Carved Rosewood Center Table, $45.

20.—Received Cash of W. D. Packard, in full of %, $————.

21.—Sold Robert Hall, on %, 1 Teacher's Desk, $25 ; 12 Dining Chairs, @ $1.75 ; 12 Cane Bottom Settees, @ $8 each.

22.—Paid Cash, Book-keeper's salary, $75 - - - - - Received Cash, in full of William Carter's note, now due, $1000.

24.—Paid Workmen, Cash to date, $193 - - - - - Sold E. A. Charlton, on %, 50 Double School-Desks, @ $9 each ; 100 Chairs for same, @ 50¢ each.

25.—Sold Wm. Johnson, for Cash, 1 Mahogany Bedstead, $20 ; 1 Marble-top Washstand, $17 - - - - - Received Cash of Robert Hall, on %, $200.

26.—Sold John S. Williams, on %, 6 Parlor Chairs, Brocatelle, @ $5 each ; 1 carved Rosewood Centre Table, $50 ; 1 Piano Stool, $10 - - - - - Paid Cash, on Drayage %, $50.

27.—Sold Peter Duff, for Cash, 6 Office Chairs, @ $2.50 each - - - - - Paid Clark Dunham, Cash in full of %, $———— - - - - - Received Cash of Robert Hall, in full of %, $————.

29.—Sold William Dallas, on %, 1 Mahogany Sofa, $35 ; 1 Rosewood Arm Chair, $45, 1 Hall Stand, $7 ; 1 Tete-a-tete, $30.

———————— NEW FIRM. ————————

July 1.—Jones and Mason have this day associated with them George F. Smith, who is to invest an equal amount with each of the former partners, and share equally in gains and losses. The value of unsold merchandise is $5500; of Tools and Implements, $750; the other resources and liabilities can be ascertained by reference to the appropriate books. Mr. Smith invests : Cash,* ———— - - - - - Bo't of Henry P. Smith, for Cash, a quantity of Pine Lumber amounting to $3500 - - - - - Paid Workmen, Cash to date, $175.

3.—Sold John S. Williams, on %, 2 Bedsteads, 1 @ $6, and 1 @ $10 ; 3 Washstands, @ $2.50 each ; 6 Kitchen Chairs, @ $1.50 each ; 1 Lounge, $15 ; 1 Secretary, $25 ; 1 Bureau, $18.

5.—Sold E. A. Trotter, for Cash, 1 Black Walnut Book-case, $60 - - - - - Sold James Thurber for Cash, 6 School Desks (single), @ $5 each ; 1 Teacher's Desk, $25 ; 2 Office Chairs, @ $7.50 each.

---

* In order to ascertain the amount of Smith's investment, it will be necessary to carry the gains to the partners' accounts.—A statement should be made similar to that on page 76.

6.—Sold Joseph Wadsworth, on his note @ 30 ds., 1 Rosewood Tete-a-tete, $65 ; 2 Ottomans, @ $10 each - - - - - Received Cash, in full of George Chrysler's note of the 2d ult., $61.

8.—Paid Workmen, Cash to date, $218 - - - - - Sold James McGrath, for Cash, 12 Dining Chairs, @ $2 each; 1 open Lounge, $17 ; 1 Bureau, $20.

10.—Received Cash, on % of Wm. Dallas, $50 - - - - - Sold Steamer Troy, on %, 2 Black Walnut Sofas, @ $45 each ; 3 Tete-a-tetes, @ $50 each ; 24 Chairs, @ $7 each.

11.—Received Cash, in full of E. A. Charlton's %, $_____ - - - - - Sold W. F. Norman for Cash, 1 Black Walnut Book-case, $60: 1 Bureau, $30 - - - - - Bo't of Robert Coons for Cash, lot of Mahogany Lumber, amounting to $5700.

15.—Paid Workmen, Cash to date, $212.

16.—Sold Henry Harper, for Cash, 50 School Desks, @ $9 each - - - - - Received Cash of John S. Williams, on %, $90.

17.—Sold Robert S. Hayward, on %, 1 Gothic Book-case, $75 - - - - - Received Cash of B. F. Butler, in full of %, $_____.

20.—Sold John S. Williams, on %, 12 Parlor Chairs, @ $5 each.

22.—Paid Workmen, Cash to date, $175.

25.—Paid Gas Bill in Cash, $15 - - - - - Sold Peter McGrath for Cash, 1 Sofa Bedstead, $50.

29.—Paid Workmen, Cash to date, $219 - - - - - Paid Cash for rent, $100.

STATEMENT,

SHOWING THE CONDITION OF THE BUSINESS JULY 31.

Resources.						
Mdse. unsold	(per Inventory),	15000				
Cash on hand,		9826	05			
Notes "		226				
W. T. Brooks,	Balance of %,	95				
John S. Williams,	" "	150	50			
Wm. Dallas,	" "	67				
Steamer Troy,	" "	408				
Robt. S. Hayward,	" "	75				
Tools and Implements, at valuation,		750		26597	55	
Liabilities.						
Wm. Jones,	Net Capital, July 1,	$8637	35			
"	⅓ Net Gain,	228	50	8865	85	
Thos. Mason,	Net Capital, July 1,	8637	35			
"	⅓ Net Gain,	228	50	8865	85	
Geo F. Smith,	Net Capital, July 1,	8637	35			
"	⅓ Net Gain,	228	50	8865	85	26597	55

95

QUESTIONS FOR REVIEW.

REMARKS, PAGE 50.

1. What is the peculiar feature of Set 3? *2.* How does the form of the Cash Book in this set differ from that in the preceding? *3.* Which is preferable? *4.* Why? *5.* For what purpose is the Sales-Book used? *6.* Is it essential that the sales should be entered on the Day-Book? *7.* How posted if not so entered? *8.* What do the initials in the margin of the Sales-Book indicate? *9.* Is the Sales-Book used in making up a list of Resources and Liabilities?

REMARKS, PAGE 72.

10. What is the purpose of Set 4? *11.* What is the important feature in this set? *12.* How does the Sales-Book differ in its use from that in Set 3? *13.* What is the advantage? *14.* What do the figures in the margin indicate? *15.* What other feature than the peculiar use of the Sales-Book is prominent in this set? *16.* How must a change in the business be marked? *17.* At what periods in business is it proper that the resources and liabilities should be shown? *18.* In admitting a new partner with an equal investment, how can the proper amount of the investment be ascertained? *19.* Why not make the new partner's investment equal to the original investment of the former proprietor?

PART II.

DOUBLE ENTRY.

PART II.

DOUBLE ENTRY.

INTRODUCTION.

If the method of keeping accounts by Single Entry may be called a *system*, that by Double Entry may with equal propriety be called a *science ;* for, while the former possesses the means of showing the *condition* of business, the latter not only affords a proof of its own correctness, but in addition to showing the condition of business, gives, with mathematical exactness, the *particular channels through which gains and losses come.* The real difference between them hinges on this latter qualification, and to the fact that in Double Entry all the results, including resources, liabilities, gains and losses, are shown in the Ledger, while in Single Entry, the partial results are gathered from various auxiliary books, including the Ledger, Cash-Book, Bill-Book, etc.

The *precise* difference may be appreciated by comparing Set 3, in Part II. with the corresponding Set in Part I., the transactions being the same in both cases.

The term *Double* Entry, as contradistinctive to *Single* Entry, has reference to the fact, that for every transaction, *two* or more entries are made in the Ledger. The condition of these entries is such that each transaction, when properly recorded, will produce on the Ledger equal debits and credits; that is, the same value which is carried to the *debtor* side of one or more accounts is also carried to the *creditor* side of one or more accounts, producing thus a perpetual equilibrium of debits and credits, and affording a distinct test of the correctness of the work.

99

The theory of "equal debits and credits" is the leading feature of Double Entry; and although its application is, in all cases, most reasonable and satisfactory to the accountant, it is often adjudged as being complex and mysterious, and calculated more to befog the mind of the uninitiated than to subserve the ends of justice.

To those who are troubled with these doubts, it is only necessary to say that Double Entry contains *every feature* of Single Entry; and, that so far as Single Entry goes, it differs in none of its *results* from Double Entry; the latter being a continuation, or rather, a *perfection* of the purposes of the former. The main distinction between the two systems is, that while in Single Entry a record is kept of *resources* and *liabilities* only, in Double Entry a similar and additional record is kept of *gains* and *losses*. This feature of Double Entry commends it at once to prudent business men; for while it may properly be regarded as affording a true indication of the comparative merits of the various schemes of profit, it also, in a great measure, guards against errors and omissions which might pass undetected in Single Entry.

As in Single, so in Double Entry, the main book of Accounts is the Ledger. The Single Entry Ledger, however, contains only accounts with individuals, while the Double Entry Ledger shows the result of each transaction, both as regards the character of the exchange and the gain or loss thereby effected. Thus accounts are kept, not only with *persons* whom we may owe, or who may owe us, but with every *species of property* in which we deal, and every *cause* producing gain or loss.

Although it is customary, in connection with Double Entry and Single Entry books alike, to keep a Cash-Book and Bill-Book, yet all the essential facts connected with cash and notes are shown in the proper Ledger accounts.

The three main books used in Double Entry are the Day-Book, Journal, and Ledger. The Day-Book and Journal are sometimes combined in one.

THE DAY-BOOK

is the original book of entry, and contains a consecutive history of the transactions, in the order and date of their occurrence. It should be plain, concise, and unequivocal in its statements; neither confusing the mind by redundancy of language, nor leaving room for doubt from lack of full explanation.

THE JOURNAL,

when used separately, is the intermediate book between the Day-Book and the Ledger. Its office is to decide upon the proper debits and credits involved in each transaction, preparatory to their going upon the Ledger. The process of thus classifying the transactions is called *journalizing.*

THE LEDGER

is the book of *results,*—the final book of entry. Here, under appropriate heads, called accounts, are arranged all the facts necessary for a full and satisfactory statement of the business; including not only an exhibition of the present resources and liabilities, but a distinct record of particular gains and losses. The process of transferring to the Ledger is called *posting.*

The following examples of these separate books, showing their characteristic records of the same transaction, will clearly indicate their use:

1.—Day-Book.

New York, January 1, 1879.

Check-mark.		Date.	Dollars.	Cents.
√	Bought of JAMES MONROE, on account,			
	500 brls. Flour . . . . @ $10		5000	
	— — — — 2 — — — —			
√	Sold ANDREW JACKSON, for Cash,			
	100 brls. Flour . . . . @ $10 50		1050	

2.—Journal.

New York, January 1, 1879. Dr.   Cr.

Ledger Page.	Ledger Titles.—*Dr.* Ledger Titles.—*Cr.*	Date.	Dollars.	Cents.	Dollars.	Cents.
1	Merchandise, *Dr.*		5000			
2	To James Monroe . . .				5000	
	— — — — 2 — — — —					
3	Cash, *Dr.*		1050			
1	To Merchandise . . .				1050	

3.—Ledger.

1

| Dr. | | | | | | | | Merchandise. | | | | | Cr. |

Month.	Day.	For what debited.	Journal Page.	Dollars.	Cents.	Month.	Day.	For what credited.	Journal Page.	Dollars.	Cents.
1879 Jan.	1	To James Monroe	1	5000		1879 Jan.	1	By Cash . . .	1	1050	

2

| Dr. | | | | | | | | James Monroe. | | | | | Cr. |

						1879 Jan.	1	By Merchandise .	1	5000	

3

| Dr. | | | | | | | | Cash. | | | | | Cr. |

1879 Jan.	1	To Merchandise .	1	1050							

THE SCIENCE OF ACCOUNTS.

ALTHOUGH the books containing a consecutive history of the business are essential for that purpose, yet the *science* of Accounts pertains exclusively to the *results* of the transactions as shown in the Ledger. Particularly is this true in Double Entry, where the Ledger contains all the results necessary for a complete rendering of the condition of the business, at any time.

Each Ledger account is, properly, a statement of some financial fact, and shows one of the four following results, viz.: a *resource*, a *liability*, a *gain*, or a *loss*. These facts or results are ascertained by taking the difference between the sides of the accounts, thus:

Dr.   Cash.   *Cr.*

Cash Received.   *Cash Paid out.*

1879					1879			
Jan.	1	To Stock (Inv't)	5000		Jan.	1	By Merchandise	2500
"	15	" Merchandise	1500		"	10	" "	1200
"	30	" "	5000		"	30	" David Brown	500
					"	"	" Expense	300
		$11500					$4500	

Total Cash Received, ... $11500
"   "   Paid out, ... 4500
Balance on hand—RESOURCE, ... $7000

Dr.   Merchandise.   *Cr.*

Outlay for Merchandise.   *Returns from Merchandise.*

1879					1879			
Jan.	1	To Cash,	2500		Jan.	15	By Cash,	1500
"	10	" "	1200		"	30	" "	5000
"	14	" David Brown,	1500				$6500	
		$5200						

Total Returns of Merchandise, ... $6500
"   Outlay for   " 5200
Net Returns—GAIN, ... $1300

103

Dr.		David Brown.						Cr.
His indebtedness to us.						*Our indebtedness to him.*		
1879 Jan.	30	To Cash,		500	1879 Jan.	14	By Merchandise,	1500

We owe him $1500
He owes us 500
Balance due him—LIABILITY, ... $1000

Dr.		Expense.						Cr.
Outlay.								
1879 Jan.	30	To Cash,		300				

Total Outlay for Expenses—LOSS, ... $300

We will suppose the above accounts to comprise all in the Ledger with the exception of the Stock, or Proprietor's account, which should represent the net investment; and that the net investment, as shown by the first entry in Cash account, is $5000. The following statement will sufficiently enforce the leading principles of the science.

Resource.—Cash on hand, ... $7000		
Liability.—We owe David Brown, ... 1000		
Net Resources, or Present Worth . .	$6000	
Gain.—On Merchandise, ... $1300		
Loss.—On Expense, ... 300		
Net Gain, ... $1000		
Add original Investment, . . . 5000		
Gives *Present Worth*, ...	$6000	

From the foregoing illustrations we deduce the following general principles:

1. An Account is a statement of facts pertaining to some person, species of property or cause, so arranged as to show some specific result.

2. Every account has two sides, a *debtor* and a *creditor ;* each containing the results of separate transactions, and showing, in the difference between the amounts, a *general* result or fact having an important bearing upon the business.

3. Accounts may be divided into two classes; one of which is used to designate the *resources* and *liabilities*, and the other, the *gains* and *losses*.

4. The net gain or net loss in business, as evinced by the general result of all the accounts showing gains or losses, is confirmed by a corresponding increase or diminution of wealth, which is shown in the general result of all the accounts showing resources or liabilities.

DEBITS AND CREDITS.

One of the great difficulties which beset the teacher of Accounts, is in the proper definition and explanation of the terms " Debit and Credit." So well is this fact appreciated, that authors have been induced to found treatises on Book-keeping upon what they regard the discovery of some "infallible rule" for journalizing, which is to revolutionize the labor and processes of instruction, and open up to the world a grand highway of "Bookkeeping-made-easy." The student is assured that the whole matter turns upon some simple fact, such, for instance, as *owing* and *being* owed. "Thus," says the author, " every *debit* owes you, and you owe every *credit ;*" and from these premises is deduced the infallible corollary, "*Debit* what owes you, and *credit* what you owe."

Other authors, again, rush to the opposite extreme, basing the theory of debits and credits upon an utter *lack* of theory, announcing, at the start, that "the items of which debits and credits are composed form a list of incongruous facts having no object in common." And yet these different theorists, widely as they may diverge touching the reasons of things, come at last to the same practical conclusion as to results.

The questions as to the *best methods* of presenting truth is a professional question, and it is the business of every author and every teacher to use the best reasons he has, and to produce the best results he can in his own way.

We believe that every student who will familiarize himself with the principles which follow, need have no difficulty in deciding upon the debits and credits involved in any business record which he may be called upon to make:

PRINCIPLES.

1.—PROPRIETORS.

The person or persons owning the business should be *credited*, under some title, for investments when made, and for their share of the gain, at such time as an accounting is made. They should also be *debited* individually for what they draw from the business— or what the business pays or assumes to pay for them—and for their share of the losses, when such losses are finally determined.

2.—CASH.

Cash account should be *debited* for all money received, and *credited* for all money paid out.

3.—OTHER PEOPLE'S WRITTEN PROMISES.

Bills Receivable account should be *debited* for all notes, drafts, or other written obligations for which we *are to receive* payment, when they become ours, and *credited* when they are paid, or otherwise disposed of.

4.—OUR WRITTEN PROMISES.

Bills Payable account should be *credited* with our written obligations when they are issued, and *debited* when they are paid or redeemed.

5.—PERSONS.

Personal accounts, or accounts with individuals, banks or other institutions competent to sue or be sued, should be *debited* under their proper titles when they become indebted to us, or we get out of their debt, and *credited* when we become indebted to them or they get out of our debt.

6.—LOSSES AND GAINS.

Causes producing losses or gains in business should be designated in accounts, bearing significant titles. Such accounts should be *debited* for all outlays or losses, and *credited* for all returns or gains.*

* This definition covers the purchase and sale of goods, the producing power of labor, the incurring of expenses, etc., etc.; in fact everything that effects an increase or diminution of wealth, or is employed to that end.

QUESTIONS FOR REVIEW.

INTRODUCTION, PAGE 99.

1. Why has Double Entry better claims to the distinction of an exact science than Single Entry? *2.* In what particulars do the two systems differ? *3.* How may the precise difference be seen? *4.* To what has the term *Double* Entry reference? *5.* What is the condition of every complete entry upon the Ledger? *6.* What is the advantage of the equilibrium produced in the Ledger? *7.* What is the main book of accounts in Double Entry? *8.* How does the Double Entry Ledger differ from the Single? *9.* What beside *personal* accounts are kept in the Double Entry Ledger? *10.* Do the Cash-Book and Bill-Book alone contain all the facts pertaining to notes and cash?— *11.* What are the three main books in Double Entry?—*12.* Which two of these are sometimes combined in one?—*13.* What does the Day-Book contain?—*14.* What should be its character?—*15.* What relation does the Journal sustain to the other books?—*16.* What is its office?—*17.* What is the process of entering in the Journal called?—*18.* Describe the Ledger.— *19.* What does the Ledger contain?—*20.* What is the process of entering in the Ledger called?

THE SCIENCE OF ACCOUNTS, PAGE 103.

21. To what does the "Science of Accounts" exclusively pertain?—*22.* Of what is each Ledger account a statement?—*23.* How are these results shown? —*24.* When the *Debit* side of Cash account is the larger, what does the difference express?—*25.* When the *Credit* side of Merchandise account is the larger, what does the difference express?—*26.* When the *Credit* side of a personal account is the larger, what does the difference express?—*27.* When the *Debit* side of Expense account is the larger, what does the difference express?—*28.* What is an Account?—*29.* What are the characteristics of an Account?—*30.* Into how many classes may Accounts be divided, and what are they?—*31.* How is the net gain or loss in business, as shown by the special accounts, confirmed?—*32.* What is one of the chief difficulties in the way of teaching accounts?—*33.* Do intelligent authors and teachers differ in their *application* of the truths of Double Entry?—*34.* When should the proprietor of the business be *debited,* and when *credited?*—*35.* When should *Cash* account be *debited,* and when *credited?*—*36.* Merchandise?—*37.* Bills Receivable?—*38.* Bills Payable?—*39.* Personal Accounts?—*40.* Expense, etc.?

ACCOUNTS CURRENT.

An Account Current in commercial usage, is the statement in proper form of a *current* or running account. It is usually made with a view to settlement and shows the balance due to or from the party to whom it is rendered. When large transactions are conducted on credit it is usual in rendering the Account Current to *average* the time of payment, so that the balance may be paid without either party losing interest. The various methods of averaging are given in most arithmetical works, and thoroughly enforced in the advanced editions of this series. We give below the most common form of an Account Current.

Mr. John R. Penn,

In Account Current with S. S. Packard.

1861						
July	1	To 2 doz. Bryant & Stratton's (H. S.) Book-keeping . .	30			
	"	1 " " " (Primary) " . .	7			
	12	6 Webster's Unabridged Dictionary . . @ $6	36			
	15	4 reams Union Letter Paper . . . . . @ $3	12			
Aug.	10	1 doz. gross Gillott's 604 Pens . . . . @ 75¢	9			
	"	20 doz. Spencerian Copy Books . . . . @ $1	20			
	15	15 Dean's Commercial Law . . . . . . @ $2	30			
	20	20 gross Spencerian Pens . . . . . . @ 75¢	15			
	"	12 reams Best Wove Cap Paper . . . . @ $4	48			
	30	50 Commercial Arithmetic . . . . . . @ 75¢	37	50		
	"	6 Robinson's Surveying . . . . @ $1.25	7	50		
	"	12 Wells' Science of Common Things . . @ 50¢	6			
	"	24 " Natural Philosophy . . . . . @ 75¢	18			
	"	24 " Chemistry . . . . @ 75¢	18		294	
		——— Cr. ———				
July	10	By Cash	10			
	15	"	145			
Aug.	1	"	50		205	
		Balance due			89	

SET 1.—DOUBLE ENTRY.

INTRODUCTORY.

DAY-BOOK, JOURNAL, AND LEDGER.

WITH EXPLANATIONS FOR JOURNALIZING, STATEMENTS, ETC.

Business Prosperous.

REMARKS.

THE following set comprises very simple transactions; the purpose being to illustrate the foregoing principles, and to initiate the student into the processes of Book-keeping. The transactions are first recorded historically in the Day-Book, in the order of their occurrence; from thence transferred to the Journal, and from thence to the Ledger. In journalizing a transaction, the first thing to be considered is, the person or thing affected; next, in what manner affected; and next, the proper application of the principle. For instance, the first entry is—" Bo't of Smith & Sons, on %, 1000 brls. Flour." The things affected are, Smith & Sons, and Flour. We have become indebted to the former, and the latter has cost an outlay. We turn to the *principles*, and learn that personal accounts should be *credited* when we become indebted to the persons (Prin. 5), and merchandise, and all species of property should be *debited* under some appropriate head for the outlay (Prin. 6). The established form of Journal entries requires the *debit* expression to precede the *credit*, and hence we have the Journal entry—" Flour Dr., Smith & Sons Cr." In posting this entry to the Leager, we open separate accounts with Flour, and Smith & Sons, debiting the former and crediting the latter. It is not really necessary that any expression should be made under the Ledger title, the date and amount being sufficient to show the result, but it is usual to insert the *opposite* Journal expression, as an explanation of the transaction. The check-mark (✓) in the Day-Book is made immediately after the transaction is carried to the Journal, and the post-mark in the margin of the Journal (indicating the Ledger page to which the account is posted), immediately upon its being posted. The numeral in the Ledger column next preceding the amounts indicates the Journal page from which the amount is tranferred. The Ledger is left in its current or *running* condition, the general results being first indicated by *pencil figures* on the smaller side of each account, and next, more completely and systematically in the Statement on page 121. The method of showing these results on the Ledger is fully shown in Set II.

New York, January 1, 1878.

√	Bought of Smith & Sons, on %,			
	1000 brls. Flour,	@ $6 00		6000
	2			
√	Sold Robert Bates, for Cash,			
	300 brls. Flour,	@ $6 50		1950
	5			
√	Sold Peter Cooper, on %,			
	250 brls. Flour,	@ $7 00		1750
	7			
√	Sold John Jones, on his Note @ 30 ds.,			
	150 brls. Flour,	@ $7 00		1050
	10			
√	Bought of J. R. Wheeler, on our Note @ 60 ds.,			
	500 bush. Wheat,	@ $1 00		500
	12			
√	Sold James Turner, for Cash,			
	100 bush. Wheat,	@ $1 25	$125 00	
	100 brls. Flour,	" 6 75	675 00	800
	14			
√	Paid Cash for Stationery and Books for use of Store,			50
	15			
√	Bought of Thomas Payne, for Cash,			
	300 brls. Flour,	@ $5 00		1500
	17			
√	Sold Patrick Murphy, for Cash,			
	100 brls. Flour,	@ $6 00		600
		Carried forward,		14200

New York, January 18, 1878.

		Brought forward,	14200	
√	Bought of George Davis, on %,			
	1000 bush. Oats, @ 75¢		750	
	————— 20 —————			
√	Sold Raymond & Co., on their Note @ 5 ds.,			
	500 bush. Oats, @ 80¢ $400 00			
	100 " Wheat, " $1 15 115 00		515	
	————— 22 —————			
√	Sold Abram Fuller, for Cash,			
	400 brls. Flour, @ $6 00 $2400 00			
	300 bush. Wheat, " 1 10 330 00		2730	
	————— 25 —————			
√	Bought of James Hathaway, on %,			
	1500 brls. Flour, @ $5 50		8250	
	————— 27 —————			
√	Sold Jonas Clark, on %,			
	1000 brls. Flour, @ $6 00		6000	
	————— 28 —————			
√	Received Cash in full for Raymond & Co.'s Note,		515	
	————— 29 —————			
√	Sold John Drummond, for Cash,			
	500 brls. Flour, @ $5 75 $2875 00			
	500 bush. Oats, " 90¢ 450 00		3325	
	————— 30 —————			
√	Paid Clerk hire, in Cash, $50 00			
	" Store rent, 50 00		100	
			36385	

New York, January 1, 1879.

		DR.	CR.
1	Flour,	6000	
2	To Smith & Sons,		6000

Flour is *debited* for outlay or cost (*Prin.* 6); Smith & Sons are *credited* because we have got in their debt (*Prin.* 5).

—————— *2* ——————

| 3 | Cash, | 1950 | |
| 1 | To Flour, | | 1950 |

Cash is *debited* because it is received (*Prin.* 2); Flour is *credited* for returns (*Prin.* 6).

—————— *5* ——————

| 4 | Peter Cooper, | 1750 | |
| 1 | To Flour, | | 1750 |

Peter Cooper is *debited* because he has got in our debt (*Prin.* 5); Flour is *credited* for returns (*Prin.* 6).

—————— *7* ——————

| 5 | Bills Receivable, | 1050 | |
| 1 | To Flour, | | 1050 |

Bills Receivable is *debited* because we have received another's written obligation (*Prin.* 3); Flour is *credited* for outlay (*Prin.* 6).

| | | 10750 | 10750 |

New York, January 10, 1878.

			DR.		CR.	
		Brought forward,	10750		10750	
6	Wheat,		500			
7		To Bills Payable,			500	
	Wheat Dr. *Prin.* 6; Bills Pay'le Cr. *Prin.* 4.					
		——— *12* ———				
3	Cash,		800			
6		To Wheat,			125	
		" Flour,			675	
	Cash Dr. *Prin.* 2; Wheat Cr. ⎫ *Prin.* 6.					
	Flour Cr. ⎬					
		——— *14* ———				
8	Expense,		50			
3		To Cash,			50	
	Expense Dr. *Prin.* 6; Cash Cr. *Prin.* 2.					
		——— *15* ———				
1	Flour,		1500			
3		To Cash,			1500	
	Flour Dr. *Prin.* 6; Cash Cr. *Prin* 2.					
		——— *17* ———				
3	Cash,		600			
1		To Flour,			600	
	Cash Dr. *Prin.* 2; Flour Cr. *Prin.* 6.					
		——— *18* ———				
9	Oats,		750			
10		To George Davis,			750	
	Oats Dr. *Prin.* 6; Geo. Davis Cr. *Prin.* 5.					
			14950		14950	

New York, January 20, 1878.

		DR.		CR.
	Brought forward,	14950		14950
5	Bills Receivable,	515		
9	To Oats,			400
6	" Wheat,			115
	Bi ls Receivable Dr., *Prin.* 3 ; Oats and Wheat Cr.. *Prin.* 6.			
	—— 22 ——			
3	Cash,	2730		
1	To Flour,			2400
6	" Wheat,			330
	Cash Dr., *Prin.* 2 ; Flour and Wheat Cr., *Prin.* 6.			
	—— 25 ——			
1	Flour,	8250		
11	To James Hathaway,			8250
	Flour Dr , *Prin.* 6 ; J. Hathaway Cr., *Prin.* 5.			
	—— 27 ——			
12	Jonas Clark,	6000		
1	To Flour,			6000
	Jonas Clark Dr., *Prin.* 5 ; Flour Cr., *Prin.* 6.			
	—— 28 ——			
3	Cash,	515		
5	To Bills Receivable,			515
	Cash Dr., *Prin.* 2. ; Bills Receivable Cr., *Prin.* 3.			
	—— 29 ——			
3	Cash,	3325		
1	To Flour,			2875
9	" Oats,			450
	Cash Dr., *Prin.* 2 ; Flour and Oats Cr., *Prin.* 6.			
	—— 30 ——			
8	Expense,	100		
3	To Cash,			100
	Expense Dr., *Prin.* 6 ; Cash Cr., *Prin.* 2.			
		36385		36385

1

Dr.			Outlay.		Flour.			Returns.		Cr.

1878						1878				
Jan.	1	To Smith & Sons,	1	6000		Jan.	2	By Cash,	1	1950
	15	Cash,	2	1500			5	P. Cooper,	1	1750
	25	J. Hathaway,	3	8250			7	Bills Rec'ble,	1	1050
		15750					12	Cash,	2	675
							17	"	"	600
		Returns, . . $17300					22	"	3	2400
		Outlay,. . . 15750					27	Jonas Clark,	3	6000
		Net returns, $1550					29	Cash,	3	2875
								17300		

2

Dr.			Our % against them.		Smith & Sons.			Their % against us.		Cr.

		We owe them $6000				1878				
						Jan.	1	By Flour,	1	6000

3

Dr.			Received.		Cash.			Paid out.		Cr.

1878						1878				
Jan.	2	To Flour,	1	1950		Jan.	14	By Expense,	2	50
	12	Wheat & Fl'r,	2	800			15	Flour,	2	1500
	17	Flour,	2	600			30	Expense,	3	100
	22	Flour & Wh't,	3	2730				1650		
	28	Bills Rec'ble,	3	515				Received, $9920		
	29	Flour,	"	3325				Paid out, 1650		
		9920						On hand, $8270		

4

Dr.			Our % against him.		Peter Cooper.			His % against us.		Cr.

1873										
Jan.	5	To Flour & Oats,	1	1750				He owes us $1750		

5

Dr.	*Others' notes received.*			Bills Rec'ble.	*Others' notes disposed of.*			Cr.

1878					1878			
Jan.	1	To Flour,	1	1050	Jan.	28	By Cash,	3	515
	20	Oats & Wh't,	3	515					
							Notes received, $1565		
			1565				" disp'd of, 515		
							" on hand, $1050		

6

Dr.	*Outlay.*			Wheat.	*Returns.*			Cr.

1878					1878			
Jan.	10	To Bills Payable,	2	500	Jan.	12	By Cash,	2	125
						20	Bills Rec'ble,	3	115
		Returns, . . . $570				22	Cash,	3	330
		Outlay, . . . 500							
		Net returns, . . $70						570	

7

Dr.	*Our notes redeemed.*			Bills Payable.	*Our notes issued.*			Cr.

					1878			
		Notes outstand'g, $500			Jan.	10	By Wheat,	2	500

8

Dr.	*Outlay.*			Expense.				Cr.

1878							
Jan.	14	To Cash,	2	50	Outlay, $150		
	30	"	3	100			
			150				

9

Dr.		Outlay.				Oats.			Returns.		Cr.
1878						1878					
Jan.	18	To Geo. Davis,	2	750		Jan.	20	By Bills Rec'ble,	2	400
							29	Cash,	3	450
		Returns, . . . $850								
		Outlay, ... 750						850		
		Net returns, . . $100								

10

Dr.	Our % against him.				George Davis.		His % against us.		Cr.
					1878				
	We owe him, $750				Jan.	18	By Oats,	2	750

11

Dr.	Our % against him.				J. Hathaway.		His % against us.		Cr.
					1878				
	We owe him, $8250				Jan.	25	By Flour,	3	8250

12

Dr.	Our % against him.				Jonas Clark.		His % against us.		Cr.
1878									
Jan.	27	To Flour,	3	6000		He owes us, $6000			

STATEMENT OF RESULTS.

WE are enabled now to exhibit the current condition of our business during the month, with the results thus far accomplished. The Ledger accounts present the following facts:—

Dr.	TRIAL BALANCE.—FACE OF LEDGER.	Cr.
15750	*Outlay.* . . . . FLOUR, . . . *Returns.*	17300
	Our % ag'st them. SMITH & SONS, . *Their % agn'st us.*	6000
9920	*Received.* . . . . CASH, ... *Paid out.*	1650
1750	*Our % ag'nst him.* PETER COOPER, *His % against us.*	
1565	*Others' notes rec'd.* BILLS REC'BLE, *Others' notes disp.of.*	515
500	*Outlay.* . . . . WHEAT, . . . *Returns.*	570
	Our notes red'm'd. BILLS PAY'BLE, *Our notes issued.* .	500
150	*Outlay.* . . . . EXPENSE, ...	
750	*Outlay.* . . . . OATS, ... *Returns.*	850
	Our % ag'nst him. GEORGE DAVIS, *His % against us.* .	750
	Our % ag'nst him. J. HATHAWAY, . *His % against us.* .	8250
6000	*Our % ag'nst him.* JONAS CLARK, . *His % against us.* .	
36385	. . . . . . *Equilibrium,*	36385

The above statement is called a "Trial Balance" for the reason most apparent; it is a *trial* to ascertain if the debits and credits on the Ledger are equal, or *balance*. It does not, as some suppose, prove the Ledger to be absolutely correct, as there are many circumstances under which the Ledger may balance, and yet be wrong. This form of Trial Balance, however, is so nearly a test that under ordinary circumstances it may be considered satisfactory. By observing the footings it will be seen that they exactly agree with those of the Journal, which could rarely be the case, were any of the Journal entries omitted in posting; and as the footings of the Journal columns also tally with that of the Day Book, it is almost conclusive that all the original entries have found their way into the Ledger. There will remain but two chances of error in the accounts, viz.: from improper Journal entries, or from posting to the wrong accounts.

In order to afford this additional test, we have found it necessary to carry into the Trial Balance the *total footings* of the Ledger. If we desired only to test the *balances*, this would not be necessary, as will be seen from the following example:

	TRIAL BALANCE.—DIFFERENCES.				Dr.	Cr.
1	FLOUR, . . .	Net Returns, . . .	Gain, . .			1550
2	SMITH & SONS, .	We owe them, . .	Liability,			6000
3	CASH, ...	Amount on hand, .	Resource,		8270	
4	PETER COOPER,	He owes us, . . .	Resource,		1750	
5	BILLS REC'BLE,	Amount on hand, .	Resource,		1050	
6	WHEAT, . . .	Net Returns, . . .	Gain, . .			70
7	BILLS PAY'BLE,	Our notes outst'g, .	Liability,			500
8	EXPENSE, . .	Outlay, ...	Loss, . .		150	
9	OATS, ...	Net Proceeds, . .	Gain, . .			100
10	GEORGE DAVIS,	We owe him, . . .	Liability,			750
11	J. HATHAWAY, .	We owe him, . . .	Liability,			8250
12	JONAS CLARK, .	He owes us, . . .	Resource,		6000	
		Equilibrium, ...			17220	17220

We have here a test of equal debits and credits quite as satisfactory as the other, and much more brief, upon the principle of *cancellation;* that is, permitting a debit to offset a credit of the same amount, and *vice versa*. These forms have each its peculiar advantages, and it is often found convenient to combine them in one. Examples of this latter method will be found in a more advanced portion of the book.

In the Trial Balance of *"Differences"* it will be seen that each Ledger account expresses one of the four results previously mentioned, viz.: a *resource*, a *liability*, a *gain*, or a *loss*. By a careful classification of these facts we are enabled to present one of the vital facts of Double Entry, viz.: that the net gain or loss in business exactly corresponds with the increase or diminution of wealth. The following will more fully illustrate this fact:

1. RESOURCES AND LIABILITIES.

	Resources.			
3	CASH,	*Amount on hand,*	$8270 00	
4	PETER COOPER,	*He owes us,*	1750 00	
5	BILLS REC'BLE,	*Notes on hand,*	1050 00	
12	JONAS CLARK,	*He owes us,*	6000 00	17070
	Liabilities.			
2	SMITH & SONS,	*We owe them,*	6000 00	
7	BILLS PAYABLE,	*Our notes outstand'g,*	500 00	
10	GEORGE DAVIS,	*We owe him,*	750 00	
11	J. HATHAWAY,	" " "	8250 00	15500
	PRESENT WORTH,			1570

2. GAINS AND LOSSES.

	Gains.			
1	Flour,	*Net Returns,*	1550 00	
6	Wheat,	" "	70 00	
9	Oats,	" "	100 00	1720
	Losses.			
8	Expense,	*Outlay,*		150
	NET GAIN,			1570

121

By comparing the numerals in these statements with those in the Trial Balance, it will be seen that *all* the Ledger accounts are used, and that the original purpose of each account is fully recognized. The statement of Gains and Losses will afford a more practical idea of the advantages of double entry than could be enforced in any other manner. The bare assertion that all *gains* are the result of an *increase,* and all *losses* of a *decrease* in wealth could not be denied; but the proof of the assertion, drawn from the Ledger itself, as indicated in the above statements, will carry conviction which must be conclusive and abiding.

Commencing business without capital, it will be easily understood that the *present worth,* or *net capital* at any time, must exactly correspond with the *net gain.*

From these illustrations we derive the following

RULES.

1.—To find the NET GAIN: *Subtract the sum of all the* LOSSES *from the sum of all the* GAINS; *or, Subtract the* CAPITAL AT COMMENCING *from the* CAPITAL AT CLOSING.

2.—To find the PRESENT WORTH: *Subtract the* LIABILITIES *from the* RESOURCES; *or, Add the* NET GAIN *to the* NET INVESTMENT.

EXAMPLES FOR PRACTICE.

EXAMPLE I.—A. commenced business with the following investment: Cash in hand, $300; Bank deposits, $4000; Merchandise, $5000; Notes, $2500. His losses and gains were as follows: Gain on mdse., $1575; Do. on Shipment speculations, $5000. Loss on expense, $300; Do. on bad debts, $1200.

What was his net gain? What his capital at the close of business?

Ans.—Net gain, $5075. Cap. at closing, $16.875.

EXAMPLE II.—B. commenced business with a cash capital of $3795.83. At the end of the year his resources and liabilities were as follows:

Resources: Mdse. unsold, $5725; Cash on hand, $3875.90; Notes, $1500;

Personal accounts, $8500. **Liabilities:** Bills payable, $8000; Personal accounts, $3500.

What is he worth at the end of the year ? How much did he gain ?

Ans.—Present worth, $8100.90.   Gain, $4305.07.

EXAMPLE III.—C. commenced business without a capital.   At the end of the year his Ledger exhibited the following balances :

	Dr.	Cr.
Cash, - - - - - - - - - - - - -	4500	
Mdse., - - - - - - - - - - - - -		1575
John Johnson, - - - - - - - - -	1500	
Robert Blake, - - - - - - - - -	1200	
Silas Burch, - - - - - - - - -		1875
Andrew Smiley, - - - - - - - - -		4725
Bills Receivable, - - - - - - - -	1900	
Bills Payable, - - - - - - - - -		1100
Expense, - - - - - - - - - - -	175	
	9275	9275

*What has been his gain ? What is his capital at the close of the year.**

EXAMPLE IV.—The following Trial Balance shows the full condition of my business at the close of a year.   Required a statement showing gains and losses, resources and liabilities.

	Dr.	Cr.	
Cash, - - - - - - - - - - - -	10397	6792	84
Merchandise, - - - - - - - - -	5000	5620	
Real Estate, - - - - - - - - -	10000	12000	
Andrew Simpson, - - - - - - - -	4000	2500	
William Matthews, - - - - - - -	8000	9750	
Expense, - - - - - - - - - -	1200		
Bills Receivable, - - - - - - -	7000	5000	
Bills Payable, - - - - - - - -		1500	
Henry Martin, - - - - - - - -	500	3434	16
Abram Guilford, - - - - - - -	1500	1000	
	47597	47597	00

* This and the succeeding example should be rendered in the form of the Statement on page 121.

PRACTICAL EXERCISES.

[To be written up after the manner of Set 1.]

TRANSACTIONS.—FIRST SERIES.

Jan. 1.—Commenced Business without Capital. Bo't of S. S. Packard on %, Mdse. amounting to $5750 - - - - - Sold John R. Penn, for Cash, 10 yds. Broadcloth, @ $5; 3 do. Vest Satin, @ $8 - - - - - Paid Cash for Stationery and Postage, $10.

2.—Sold J. H. Goldsmith, on %, 1 Vest Pattern, $7.50; Trimmings for same, $2; 50 yds. Amoskeag Sheeting, @ 12¢.

3.—Sold J. M. Bradstreet, on his note @ 60 ds., 1 case Boots, 24 pairs, @ $3.50; 25 yds. Flannel, @ 50¢ - - - - - Sold E. A. Charlton, for Cash, 1 box Hosiery, $10; 75 yds. Lowell Prints, @ 10¢.

5.—Paid S. S. Packard, Cash on %, $50.

7.—Sold Robert Baker, invoice of Shirting and Fancy Cloths, for $3700; Received in payment, Cash, $3000; Balance charged on %.

9.—Paid store rent in Cash, $100 - ⫻ - - Received Cash in full of J. H. Goldsmith's %, $——.

10.—Sold James S. Packard, on %, 20 yds. Broadcloth, @ $3.75; 50 do. Cassimeres, @ $1.

12.—Sold C. J. Dietrich, for Cash, 12 pairs Ladies' Congress Gaiters, @ $2; 1 case Misses' Tipped Shoes, 24 pairs, $1.25; 3 cases Men's Double sole Boots, 36 pairs, @ $4.

14.—Paid Clerk's Salary in Cash, $50 - - - - - Sold J. C. Bailey, for Cash, 1 doz. Balmoral Skirts, 12 @ $2; 1 piece Mous. de Laine, 75 yds., @ 20¢; 1 do. Wamsutta Sheeting, 50 yds., @ 10¢.

15.—Bo't of James Dawes, on our note @ 3 mos., invoice of Fancy Broadcloth, amounting to $2500 - - - - - Sold Rob't C. Spencer, for Cash, 2 pieces Broadcloth, 50 yds., @ $3.50; 1 do. Lowell Prints, 25 yds., @ 12¢.

16.—Paid S. S. Packard, Cash on %, $2000 - - - - - Sold Henry Ivison, on %, 150 yds. Wamsutta Sheeting, @ 15¢; 50 yds. Broadcloth, @ $4.

18.—Received Cash of James S. Packard, in full of %, ——- - - - Sold Richmond Kingman, for Cash, 3 doz. Elastic Hoop Skirts, 36 @ $2; 4 doz. Balmoral do., 48 @ $2.25.

124

20.—Sold Henry Blakeman, for Cash, 1 piece Irish Linen, 50 yds., @ 75¢; 3 do. Lowell Prints, 150 yds., @ 10¢; 5 do. Amoskeag Sheeting, 250 yds., @ 14¢.

21.—Sold J. C. Bryant, on %, 2 cases Ladies' Tipped Gaiters, 48 pairs, @ $2; 5 do. Boys' Double-sole Boots, 60 pairs, @ $1.50.

22.—Paid Cash for petty expenses, $15.50.

25.—Rec'd Cash on Robert Baker's %, $350 ----- Paid S. S. Packard, Cash on %, $500 ------ Sold Lorenzo Fairbanks, on %, 50 yds. Broadcloth, @ $4; 75 do. Cassimeres, @ $1.25.

27.—Sold James Smith, for Cash, 3 pieces Cambric Muslin, 60 yds., @ 25¢; 3 do. Scotch Plaid, 120 yds., @ 11¢ ----- Sold J. McMillan, on his note @ 30 ds., 40 yds. Black Doeskin, @ $1.25; 8 pieces Merrimack Prints, 250 yds., @ 10¢.

30.—Sold Peter McGrath, for Cash, our entire stock of goods, amounting, per Inventory, to $3450 ----- Paid S. S. Packard, in full of %, $3200.

Trial Balance.

The following Trial Balance shows the condition of the Ledger accounts after writing up the foregoing transactions.

The student should render his statement therefrom after the manner of the statement, Set I.

Face of Ledger.	Dr.		Cr.	
2 S. S. Packard, - - - - - - - - - - -	5750		5750	
1 Merchandise, - - - - - - - - - -	8250		8971	45
3 Cash, - - - - - - - - - - - - -	7747	70	5925	50
4 Expense, - - - - - - - - - - -	175	50		
5 J. H. Goldsmith, - - - - - - - -	15	50	15	50
6 Bills Receivable, - - - - - - - -	171	50		
7 Robert Baker, - - - - - - - - -	700		350	
8 James S. Packard, - - - - - - -	125		125	
9 Bills Payable, - - - - - - - -			2500	
10 Henry Ivison, - - - - - - - - -	222	50		
11 J. C. Bryant, - - - - - - - - -	186			
12 L. Fairbanks, - - - - - - - - -	293	75		
	23637	45	23637	45

SET 2.—DOUBLE ENTRY.

(In Colors.)

DAY-BOOK, JOURNAL, LEDGER, AND AUXILIARIES.

LEDGER CLOSED, AND RESULTS SHOWN IN AN IMPROVED FORM OF BALANCE SHEET, WITH FULL EXPLANATIONS.

Prosperous.

REMARKS.

This set is a continuation of Set 1, although the nature of the business undergoes a change. The merchandise represented in the previous set being all disposed of, we now invest in a more miscellaneous stock, comprising a general assortment of groceries and provisions. Instead of keeping a distinct account with each article of traffic, as in Set 1, we classify all under the title of " Merchandise." This is the usual business method, and should always be adopted, except where it is essential to know the gains and losses on each particular kind of property.

Having a net capital at commencement, the first entry must pertain to the existing resources and liabilities. Stock, or the proprietor, is credited with the total investment, and debited with the liabilities assumed, according to Principle 1.

The term "Sundries" is here, for the first time, used in its technical sense. It means *sundry accounts*, or sundry items, and is convenient as a Journal expression, and to avoid the necessity of enumerating the items which comprise the totals carried to the Ledger accounts. This convenience will be immediately apparent by comparing the Ledger entries of this set with those of the preceding.

The object and method of "closing the Ledger" is also fully illustrated; a point which the student should not pass lightly over. The great difficulty in learning the science of Accounts from a text-book, exists in the tendency to *copy* the forms and exercises mechanically without a proper understanding of the principles.

The business aspect presented by the forms of this set, will at once commend them to the student, as models for his emulation. The *red ink* entries, in particular, are intended to remove all the obstacles to a full and clear understanding of the instructions given.

In short, Set 2 is presented as embracing, in completeness, the essential qualities of Double Entry; and as such, it is commended to careful attention.

New York, February 1, 1880.

Commenced Business this day with the following Resources and Liabilities, taken from previous Ledger:

———— RESOURCES. ————

Cash on hand,	$8270 00	
Notes and Drafts,	1050 00	
Peter Cooper's account,	1750 00	
Jonas Clark's "	6000 00	17070

———— LIABILITIES. ————

Notes outstanding,	$500 00	
Smith & Sons' account,	6000 00	
George Davis, "	750 00	
James Hathaway's "	8250 00	15500

"

BOUGHT OF COMSTOCK & CO., for Cash,

10 hhds. N. O. Mol., 600 gal.,	@ 40¢	$240 00	
10 " Cuba Sug., 9500 lbs.,	" 5¢	475 00	
17 bags Rio Coffee, 1575 "	" 16¢	252 00	
20 hf. ch. Ool. Tea, 1080 "	" 50¢	540 00	
10 tierces Rice, 5000 "	" 4½¢	225 00	1732

2

SOLD S. S. RANDALL, on %,

3 gals. Molasses,	@ 50¢	$1 50		
200 lbs. Sugar,	" 6¢	12 00		
150 " Coffee,	" 16¢	24 00	37	50

3

SOLD JAMES W. LUSK, on his Note @ 30 ds.,

2 hhds. Sugar, 2100 lbs.,	@ 6¢	$126 00	
10 hf. chests Tea, 540 lbs.,	" 55¢	297 00	423

"

PAID CASH TO GEO. DAVIS in full of %.	750	
	35512	50

New York, February 4, 1880.

		Amount forward,	35512	50
√	SOLD HENRY C. SPENCER, on %,			
	2 hhds. Molasses, 120 gals., @ 45¢		54	

——————— 5 ———————

	BOUGHT OF J. A. TILFORD, on our Note @ 60 ds.,			
√	10 tubs Lard, 400 lbs., @ 13¢	52 00		
	20 boxes Soap, 1400 lbs., " 7¢	98 00		
	5 brls. Pork, 1000 lbs., " 10¢	100 00	250	

——————— " ———————

	SOLD HARMER SMITH, for Cash,			
√	2 brls. Pork, 400 lbs., @ 10½¢	42 00		
	1 tierce Rice, 500 lbs., " 5¢	25 00	67	

——————— 6 ———————

	SOLD B. F. CARPENTER, on %,			
√	2 tierces Rice, 1000 lbs., @ 5½¢	55 00		
	1 bag Rio Coffee, 150 lbs., " 18¢	27 00	82	

——————— " ———————

	BOUGHT OF CLARENCE DOUBLEDAY, for Cash,			
√	10 brls. Potatoes, @ $3 00	30 00		
	1000 lbs. Eng. Dairy Cheese, " 18¢	180 00	210	

——————— 7 ———————

	SOLD JAMES REED, for Cash,			
√	10 lbs. Coffee, @ 18¢	1 80		
	3 boxes Soap, 210 lbs., " 8¢	16 80	18	60

——————— 8 ———————

	BOUGHT OF ROBERT HANAFORD, for Cash,			
√	10 hhds. Hav. Sugar, 11000 lbs., @ 5¢	550 00		
	3 " N. O. " 3700 " " 5½¢	203 50	753	50

——————— 9 ———————

	SOLD HENRY VAN DYCK, on %,			
√	2 hhds. Havana Sugar, 1970 lbs., @ 6¢		118	20
			37065	80

DOUBLE ENTRY—DAY-BOOK.

New York, February 10, 1880.

	Amount forward,		37065	80
PAID JAMES HATHAWAY, Cash on %,			4000	
12				
SOLD JAMES HATHAWAY, on %,				
1 brl. Pork, 200 lbs.,	@ 11¢	$22 00		
1 bag Rio Coffee, 110 lbs.,	" 18¢	19 80		
1 hhd. Hav. Sugar, 900 lbs.,	" 6¢	54 00	95	80
13				
SOLD L. FAIRBANKS, on %,				
100 lbs. Eng. Dairy Cheese,	@ 25¢	$25 00		
1 brl. Potatoes,		4 00	29	
14				
SOLD HENRY VAN DYCK, on %,				
10 lbs. Coffee,	@ 18¢	$1 80		
50 " Eng. Dairy Cheese,	" 25¢	12 50		
50 " Rice,	" 5½¢	2 75	17	05
15				
PAID CASH for rent of store,			100	
"				
SOLD J. T. CALKINS, for Cash,				
150 lbs. Eng. Dairy Cheese,	@ 25¢		37	50
17				
REC'D CASH OF HENRY C. SPENCER, in full of %,			54	
18				
SOLD S. S. RANDALL, on %,				
25 lbs. Tea,	@ 56¢	$14 00		
50 " Lard,	" 15¢	7 50		
20 " Rice,	" 5¢	1 00	22	50
20				
SOLD PETER COOPER, on %,				
2 brls. Pork, 400 lbs.,	@ 11¢		44	
			41465	65

New York, February 22, 1880.

		Amount forward,	41465	65
SOLD E. F. HILL, on %,				
1 hf. chest Tea, 54 lbs.,	@ 60¢		32	40

----------------- *23* -----------------

RECEIVED OF JONAS CLARK, in full of %,				
Cash,		$3000 00		
Note, @ 90 ds.,		3000 00	6000	

----------------- *25* -----------------

PAID SMITH & SONS, Cash on %,	3000	

----------------- *"* -----------------

SOLD GEORGE DAVIS, on %,				
2 hhds. N. O. Molasses, 120 gal.,	@ 44⅔¢		53	60

----------------- *26* -----------------

PAID CASH for our note, favor of J. R. WHEELER,	500	

----------------- *"* -----------------

SOLD E. C. BRADFORD, for Cash,				
10 lbs. Rio Coffee,	@ 19¢	$1 90		
10 " Tea,	" 50¢	5 00		
50 " Rice,	" 7¢	3 50	10	40

----------------- *27* -----------------

SOLD EDWIN MORGAN, for Cash,				
1 tierce Rice, 500 lbs.,	@ 6¢	$30 00		
2 brls. Potatoes,	" 3 00	6 00	36	

----------------- *28* -----------------

PAID CLERK'S SALARY, in Cash,			100	
			51198	05

Double Entry—Journal.

1

New York, February 1, 1880.

		Dr.		Cr.	
1	SUNDRIES, To STOCK,			17070	
5	CASH,	8270			
2	BILLS RECEIVABLE,	1050			
3	PETER COOPER,	1750			
4	JONAS CLARK,	6000			
	"				
1	STOCK, To SUNDRIES,	15500			
7	" BILLS PAYABLE,			500	
8	" SMITH & SONS,			6000	
9	" GEORGE DAVIS,			750	
10	" J. HATHAWAY,			8250	
	"				
6	MERCHANDISE,	1732			
5	To CASH,			1732	
	2				
11	S. S. RANDALL,				
6	To MERCHANDISE,	37	50	37	50
	3				
2	BILLS RECEIVABLE,	423			
6	To MERCHANDISE,			423	
	"				
9	GEORGE DAVIS,	750			
5	To CASH,			750	
	4				
12	HENRY C. SPENCER,	54			
6	To MERCHANDISE,			54	
	5				
6	MERCHANDISE,	250			
7	To BILLS PAYABLE,			250	
	"				
5	CASH,	67			
6	To MERCHANDISE,			67	
		35883	50	35883	50

New York, February 6, 1880.

		DR.		CR.	
17 6	B. F. CARPENTER, *Amounts forward,* To MERCHANDISE,	35883 82	50	35883 82	50
6 5	MERCHANDISE, " To CASH,	210		210	
5 6	CASH, 7 To MERCHANDISE,	18	60	18	60
6 5	MERCHANDISE, 8 To CASH,	753	50	753	50
13 6	HENRY VAN DYCK, 9 To MERCHANDISE,	118	20	118	20
10 5	JAMES HATHAWAY, 10 To CASH,	4000		4000	
10 6	JAMES HATHAWAY, 12 To MERCHANDISE,	95	80	95	80
14 6	L. FAIRBANKS, 13 To MERCHANDISE,	29		29	
13 6	HENRY VAN DYCK, 14 To MDSE.,	17	05	17	05
15 5	EXPENSE, 15 To CASH,	100		100	
5 6	CASH, " To MERCHANDISE,	37	50	37	50
		41345	15	41345	15

New York, February 17, 1880.

			DR.		CR.	
		Amounts forward,	41345	15	41345	15
5	CASH,		54			
12		To H. C. SPENCER,			54	
		18				
11	S. S. RANDALL,		22	50		
6		To MERCHANDISE,			22	50
		20				
3	PETER COOPER,		44			
6		To MERCHANDISE,			44	
		22				
16	E. F. HILL,		32	40		
6		To MERCHANDISE,			32	40
		23				
4	SUNDRIES,	To JONAS CLARK,			6000	
5	CASH,		3000			
2	BILLS RECEIVABLE,		3000			
		25				
8	SMITH & SONS,		3000			
5		To CASH,			3000	
		"				
9	GEORGE DAVIS,		53	60		
6		To MERCHANDISE,			53	60
		26				
7	BILLS PAYABLE,		500			
5		To CASH,			500	
		"				
5	CASH,		10	40		
6		To MERCHANDISE,			10	40
		27				
5	CASH,		36			
6		To MERCHANDISE,			36	
		28				
15	EXPENSE,		100			
6		To CASH,			100	
			51198	05	51198	05

1

Dr.						Stock.				Cr.	
1880			1			1880			1		
Feb.	28	To Sundries, *Balance,*	L19	15500 *2103*	*05*	Feb.	1 28	By Sundries, Loss & Gain,	L5	17070 533	05
				17603	05					17603	05

2

Dr.					Bills Receivable.				Cr.
1880			1		1880				
Feb.	1 3 23	To Stock, Mdse., J. Clark,	1 1 3	1050 423 3000	Feb.	28	*By Balance,*	L19	*4473*
				4473					4473

3

Dr.					Peter Cooper.				Cr.
1880			1		1880				
Feb.	1 20	To Stock, Mdse.,	3	1750 44	Feb.	28	*By Balance.*	L19	*1794*
				1794					1794

4

Dr.					Jonas Clark.				Cr.
1880			1		1880			3	
Feb.	1	To Stock,		6000	Feb.	23	By Sundries,		6000

5

Dr. | Cash. | **Cr.**

1880						1880					
Feb.	1	To Stock,	1	8270		Feb.	1	By Mdse.,	1	1732	
"	5	" Mdse.,	"	67		"	3	" Geo. Davis,	"	750	
"	7	" "	2	18	60	"	6	" Mdse.,	2	210	
"	15	" "	"	37	50	"	8	" "	"	753	50
"	17	" H. C. Spencer,	3	54		"	10	" J. Hathaway,	"	4000	
"	23	" Jonas Clark,	"	3000		"	15	" Expense,		100	
"	26	" Mdse.,	"	10	40	"	25	" Smith & Sons,	3	3000	
"	27	" "	"	36		"	26	" Bills Payable,	"	500	
						"	28	" Expense,	"		
						"	"	" *Balance,*	L19	*348*	
				11493	50					11493	50

6

Dr. | Merchandise. | **Cr.**

1880						1880					
Feb.	1	To Cash,	1	1732		Feb.	2	By S. S. Randall,	1	37	50
"	5	" Bills Payable,	"	250		"	3	" Bills Rec'ble,	"	423	
"	6	" Cash,	2	210		"	4	" H. C. Spencer,	"	54	
"	8	" "	"	753	50	"	5	" Cash,	"	67	
"	28	" *Loss & Gain,*	L18	*733*	*05*	"	6	" B. F. Carpent'r	2	82	
						"	7	" Cash,	"	18	60
						"	9	" H. Van Dyck,	"	118	20
						"	12	" J. Hathaway,	"	95	80
						"	13	" L. Fairbanks,	"	29	
						"	14	" H. Van Dyck,	"	17	05
						"	15	" Cash,	"	37	50
						"	18	" S. S. Randall,	3	22	50
						"	20	" Peter Cooper,	"	44	
						"	23	" E. F. Hill,	"	32	40
						"	25	" Geo. Davis,	"	53	60
						"	26	" Cash,	"	10	40
						"	27	" "	"	36	
						"	28	" *Balance (Inv.),*	L19	*2500*	
				3678	55					3678	55

7

Dr.							Bills Payable.			Cr.	
1880						1880					
Feb.	26	To Cash,	3	500		Feb.	1	By Stock,	1	500	
	28	*Balance,*	L19	*250*			5	Mdse.,	1	250	
				750						750	

8

Dr.							Smith & Sons.			Cr.	
1880						1880					
Feb.	25	To Cash,	3	3000		Feb.	1	By Stock,	1	6000	
	28	*Balance,*	L19	*3000*							
				6000						6000	

9

Dr.							George Davis.			Cr.	
1880						1880					
Feb.	3	To Cash,	1	750		Feb.	1	By Stock,	1	750	
Feb.	25	To Mdse.,	3	53	60	Feb.	28	*By Balance,*	L19	*53*	*60*

10

Dr.							James Hathaway.			Cr.	
1880						1880					
Feb.	10	To Cash,	2	4000		Feb.	1	By Stock,	1	8250	
	12	Mdse.,	1	95	80						
	28	*Balance,*	L19	*4154*	*20*						
				8250	00					8250	

DOUBLE ENTRY—LEDGER.

11

Dr.   S. S. Randall.   **Cr.**

1880						1880				
Feb.	2	To Mdse.,	1	37	50	Feb.	28	By Balance,	L19	60
"	18	" "	3	22	50					
				60						60

12

Dr.   Henry C. Spencer.   **Cr.**

1880					1880				
Feb.	4	To Mdse.,	1	54	Feb.	17	By Cash,	3	54

13

Dr.   Henry Van Dyck.   **Cr.**

1880						1880					
Feb.	9	To Mdse.,	2	118	20	Feb.	28	By Balance,	L19	135	25
"	14	" "	"	17	05						
				135	25					135	25

14

Dr.   L. Fairbanks.   **Cr.**

1880					1880				
Feb.	13	To Mdse.	2	29	Feb.	28	By Balance,	L19	29

15

Dr.   Expense.   **Cr.**

1880					1880				
Feb.	15	To Cash,	2	100	Feb.	28	By Loss & Gain,	L18	200
"	28	" "	3	100					
				200					200

16

Dr.						E. F. Hill.						Cr.
1880 Feb.	22	To Mdse.,	3	32	40	1880 Feb.	28	By Balance,	L19	32	40	

17

Dr.					B. F. Carpenter.						Cr.
1880 Feb.	6	To Mdse.,	2	82	1880 Feb.	28	By Balance,	L19	82		

18

Dr.						Loss and Gain.						Cr.
1880 Feb.	28	To Expense,	L15	200		1880 Feb.	28	By Mdse.,	L6	735	05	
	"	Stock,	L1	533	05							
				733	05					733	05	

19

Dr.		Resources.					Balance.	Liabilities.				Cr.
1880 Feb.	28	To Mdse.,	L6	2500		1880 Feb.	28	By Bills Payable,	L7	250		
	"	Bills Rec'ble,	L2	4473			"	Smith & Sons,	L8	3000		
	"	P. Cooper,	L3	1794			"	J. Hathaway,	L10	4154	20	
	"	Cash,	L5	348			"	Stock,	L1	2103	05	
	"	Geo. Davis,	L9	53	60							
	"	S. S. Randall,	L11	60								
	"	H. Van Dyck,	L13	135	25							
	"	L. Fairbanks,	L14	29								
	"	E. F. Hill,	L16	32	40							
	"	B. F. Carpen'r	L17	82								
				9507	25					9507	25	

S. S. PACKARD'S BALANCE SHEET.*

Taken February 28, 1880.

Account	L. Fol.	Trial Balance Dr.	Trial Balance Cr.	Inventory	Business Accounts Losses	Business Accounts Gains	Stock Dr.	Stock Cr.	Financial Statement Resources	Financial Statement Liabilities
Stock	1	15500	17070					1570		
Bills Receivable	2	4473							4473	
Peter Cooper	3	1794							1794	
Cash	5	11493 50	11145						348 50	
Merchandise	6	2945 50	1178 55	2500		733 05			2500	
Bills Payable	7	500	750							250
Smith & Sons	8	3000	6000							3000
George Davis	9	803 60	750						53 60	
James Hathaway	10	4095 80	8820							4154 20
S. S. Randall	11	60							60	
Henry Van Dyck	13	135 25							135 25	
L. Fairbanks	14	60							60	
Expense	15	200			200					
E. F. Hill	16	33 40							33 40	
B. F. Carpenter	17	82							82	
To Stock—Net Gain					533 05			533 05		
To Balance—Net Capital							2103 05			2103 05
		45144 05	45144 05		733 05	733 05	2103 05	2103 05	9507 25	9507 25

* For full instructions in preparing this Balance Sheet, see page 147.

141

ORDER AND PURPOSE OF CLOSING THE LEDGER.

In the preceding set it was thought best to leave the Ledger in its open or current condition, the *results* of the business being shown in a separate statement. When the object is to know simply the condition of the business, this method is sufficient; but when it becomes necessary to mark the progress of the business in some enduring manner upon the Ledger, the accounts must be "closed," and the *balances* exhibited, either under the account itself, or in some other account, of similar import. From the statement in connection with the previous set, the student has learned that the Double Entry Ledger contains *two* classes of accounts; one showing the *present condition* of the business, by representing all its *resources* and *liabilities,* and the other showing its *progress,* by representing its particular *gains* and *losses.* For the purpose of distinction, and as a proper designation of their character, we designate the former of these classes, FINANCIAL, and the latter BUSINESS accounts. By FINANCIAL accounts, therefore, is meant those which show the financial condition; and by BUSINESS, those which show the progressive steps and characteristics of the business. The student who has acquired the foregoing instructions, will have no difficulty in making this classification.

The object of "closing" the Ledger is to put an end to its current condition by absorbing the BUSINESS accounts; for inasmuch as the proprietor is to be credited with his net investment, whenever that net investment is increased by gains, his account should get the benefit of it. As it would be impracticable to carry the separate gains and losses to the proprietor's account when they accrue, they are permitted to remain in the accounts producing them, until such periods as may be deemed best to transfer them. This is usually done once a year, and in some establishments every six months, thus making an era in the business, and restoring the Ledger to its proper condition of showing only resources and liabilities.

PROCESS OF CLOSING.

It is supposed that the student has gone through with the labor of journalizing and posting the transactions in Set 2, and that his Ledger accounts present an equilibrium of debits and credits. To test this fact, before proceeding farther, we will take an abstract of the Ledger technically called a

Dr.   TRIAL BALANCE.   *Cr.*

Differences.		Face of Ledger.			Face of Ledger.		Differences.	
		15500		. . . Stock	17070		1570	
4473		4473		. . . Bills Receivable . .				
1794		1794		. . . Peter Cooper . .				
		6000		. . . Jonas Clark	6000			
348		11493	50	. . . Cash	11145	50		
1766	95	2945	50	. . . Merchandise	1178	55		
		500		. . . Bills Payable . . .	750		250	
		3000		. . . Smith & Sons . . .	6000		3000	
53	60	803	60	. . . George Davis . . .	750			
		4095	80	. . . James Hathaway .	8250		4154	20
60		60		. . . S. S. Randall . .				
		54		. . . Henry C. Spencer	54			
135	25	135	25	. . . Henry Van Dyck . .				
29		29		. . . L. Fairbanks				
200		200		. . . Expense				
32	40	32	40	. . . E. F. Hill				
82		82		. . . B. F. Carpenter . .				
8974	20	51198	05	. . . *Equilibrium*	51198	05	8974	20

The above is the most comprehensive form of the Trial Balance, and one to be commended for its utility. It will be seen that the footings of the "Face of Ledger" columns exactly agree with the footings of the Day-Book and Journal; which affords evidence that all the transactions have found their way to the Ledger. The columns of "Differences," which must also balance. afford a test of the results of each account.

Having satisfied ourselves that the transactions have been properly posted, we now proceed to close the Ledger accounts. It must not be forgotten that the object of closing the Ledger is to present, in a proper manner, both the *present condition* of our business and its *progress*. Its present condition can be shown by a list of its resources and liabilities; and its progress by a list of its gains and losses.

By a careful examination of the facts, it will be seen that *resources* are shown by an excess of the *debit* side of FINANCIAL accounts, and *liabilities* by an excess of the *credit* side of FINANCIAL accounts; and that *losses* are shown by an excess of the *debit* side of BUSINESS accounts, and *gains* by an excess of the *credit* side of BUSINESS accounts. This will suggest the propriety of opening two accounts for these general results: one to contain the resources and liabilities, and the other the gains and losses. We will now open these accounts under the titles of "Loss and Gain," and "Balance," the former to contain the results of the BUSINESS accounts, and the latter of the FINANCIAL accounts. Before proceeding to close the accounts, we must see if they are all in a condition to show the results desired. The Merchandise account, as it now stands, shows an excess of the debit side, and would therefore represent a *loss,* if the merchandise were all sold. The account itself does not show whether the property is all sold; and the only means of ascertaining the facts in the case, is to take an actual inventory, or a valuation of that which remains unsold. When this value is ascertained, the Merchandise account should be credited with it, and Balance account debited. The Merchandise account will then be competent to show the gain or loss on merchandise. We have estimated the unsold merchandise in this case to be worth $2500, which amount we enter on the credit side of Merchandise account in *red ink,** and transfer the same immediately to Balance account, The accounts are now in a condition to close; and we will take them in their order. The first account (after stock, which is the proprietor's own account) is Bills Receivable. This account represents a resource consisting of other people's notes on hand; the debit side showing the notes received, and the credit side those disposed of, if any. We *close* the account by entering the difference, *in red ink,* on the *credit* side, and footing up the sides, drawing double red lines underneath. The red ink entry, or *balance,* is

---

* An entry in *red ink* on the Ledger, denotes that the amount thus written *is to be transferred*, either to some other account, or to another position under the same account. It also shows that the entry is *first* made in the Ledger, not having passed through the usual preliminary books of entry. Red ink entries are always transferred to the *opposite side* from where they are first written, for the reason that they indicate an excess of that side.

transferred immediately to the *debit* side of Balance account. The next account, Peter Cooper, is closed in the same way. The next, Jonas Clark, already balances, and we close it by simply ruling the double red lines. The next, Cash account, is closed in the same manner as Bills Receivable, the balance being transferred as a resource to Balance account. The Merchandise account shows a *gain*, and the balance is transferred to the *credit* side of Loss and Gain account. Bills Payable account shows a *liability*, and the balance is transferred to the *credit* side of Balance account. Smith & Son's account also shows a *liability*, and the balance is transferred to the *credit* side of Balance account. George Davis' account shows a *resource*, and the balance is transferred to the *debit* side of Balance account. James Hathaway's account shows a *liability*, and is transferred to the *credit* of Balance. S. S. Randall's, Henry Van Dyck's, and L. Fairbank's accounts, all show *resources*, and are transferred to the *debit* side of Balance. Expense account shows a *loss*, and is transferred to the *debit* side of Loss and Gain. E. F. Hill's and B. F. Carpenter's accounts both show a *resource*, and are transferred to the *debit* of Balance.

We have now the *results* of all the accounts exhibited under the heads of Loss and Gain and Balance, and if the balances have been properly transferred, these accounts, together with the (unclosed) Stock account, must be in equilibrium. To test this, we next take a Trial Balance of these three accounts, which we call the

SECOND TRIAL BALANCE.	Dr.		Cr.	
Stock - - - - - - - - - - - - -	15500		17070	
Loss and Gain - - - - - - - - -	200		733	05
Balance - - - - - - - - - - - -	9507	25	7404	20
	25207	25	25207	25

Having thus satisfied ourselves that the balances have been properly transferred, we now proceed to accomplish the grand object of closing the Ledger, by carrying the net gain from the Loss and Gain to the Stock account. The Stock account now contains the capital invested increased by the gain, which must, of course, equal the *present worth*, as shown by the Balance account. We now close Stock account into Balance, which must produce an equilibrium of the Balance account, and complete, in that account, the record of resources and liabilities.

The Balance account is used in these sets for its convenience in collecting, under one title, all the resources and liabilities. The same effect may be produced by bringing down the balances under the financial accounts. This latter method is adopted in business, and particularly where the record is continued in the same Ledger.

From these remarks and applications we are prepared to submit the following order of closing the Ledger, which the student will do well to observe particularly, and to follow out in practice.

ORDER OF CLOSING.

First.—Open an account with "Loss and Gain" (if not already opened), and another with "Balance," the former to contain the *losses* and *gains*, and the latter the *resources* and *liabilities*.

Second.—Ascertain from the inventory if any property remains unsold; and if so, credit each account for which such property was originally debited, with the value of that unsold, making the entry in *red ink*, "By Balance," and transfer the amount directly to the debit side of Balance account, making this entry in *black ink*, "To Merchandise," or "To Real Estate," or any other account from which the amount is transferred. The Ledger accounts will each show, now, one of the four following results, viz.: a Resource, a Liability, a Gain, or a Loss.

Third.—Omitting Stock (or the Partners' accounts), commence with the first account in the Ledger. First ascertain which of the above results it shows, and make the closing entry accordingly. If the difference represent a resource or a liability, enter upon the smaller side, in *red ink*, "To," or "By Balance," as the case may be, and transfer the amount in *black ink* to the opposite side of the Balance account. If the difference represent a gain or loss, enter on the smaller side in red ink "To" or "By Loss and Gain," and transfer the amount in the same manner to Loss and Gain account. Close all the accounts (except Stock or Partners'), and transfer the balances as directed. The Loss and Gain account will now show on the debit side all the losses, and on the credit side all the gains, the difference being the net loss or net gain. The Balance account will show on the debit side all the resources, and on the credit side all the liabilities, the difference being the real interest or present investment of the proprietor or proprietors.

Fourth.—Take a second Trial Balance, or a Trial Balance of the remaining open accounts: Stock (or Partners'), Loss and Gain, and Balance. If the balances have been properly transferred, the debits and credits of these accounts taken together must be equal.

Fifth.—Close Loss and Gain account into Stock, or, if it be a partnership business, into the partners' accounts, dividing the gain or loss, according to agreement. The Stock or Partners' accounts will now show the original investment increased by the gain, or decreased by the loss; the difference being the *present* net investment. Inasmuch as the Balance account shows the same thing, they must, of course, agree.

Sixth.—Close Stock (or Partners' accounts) into Balance account, which must equalize that account, it showing now, on one side, the total resources, and on the other side the total liabilities, and presenting, in the most condensed form, the exact present condition of the business.

BALANCE SHEETS.

IN commercial usage a "Balance Sheet" signifies the systematic arrangement of facts, for the purpose of exhibiting at a view the condition of business. The forms in use are various, according to the necessities of the occasion or the ingenuity of the accountant. Of these the example given on page 141 comprises the most complete and symmetrical of which we have a knowledge. The following explanation will be found serviceable in preparing this sheet for the entries :

1. Take a sheet of paper of proper size, and for a border, if such is desired, rule double red lines around the margin.

2. Rule the parallel head-lines, leaving proper space for double captions, as in the example.

3. Ascertain the number of Ledger accounts to be represented; which will embrace all the accounts in the Trial Balance that do not cancel.* If the business is that of a single proprietor, usually called "Stock" business, rule in pencil as many lines as

---

* Should there be a large number of personal accounts, it will be found difficult to include them all *separately* in this form. In such case it is customary to employ the two general titles, "Accounts Receivable," and "Accounts Payable," the one embracing all amounts owing *to* us on personal account, and the other all amounts owing *by* us. This curtailment will enable the facts of any common business to be shown in this form.

will contain all the accounts and *five* additional. If it be a partnership business with two or more partners, rule three additional lines for each partner; thus, for "Stock" business, *five* lines more than all the accounts; for two partners, *eight* lines more than all the accounts; for three partners, *eleven* lines more, and so on.

4. Lay off proper spaces for debit and credit money columns; first for the footings of Ledger Accounts, second for Gains and Losses, third for Stock, or if partners, for each partner—and fourth for Resources and Liabilities; also, for a *single* money column for Inventories, and for Ledger titles and their Ledger folios. The position of these columns will be seen in the example given. These spaces can best be appropriated by using a pair of dividers, and giving each of the captions its just proportions.

5. After denoting the proper space for each heading, which can best be done with pencil, commence to rule in red ink at the right hand and bring all the lines of the two captions, "Real Accounts" and "Stock," or one of the partners, down to the lower pencil line. For the other partners drop two lines. For Losses and Gains drop two lines in Stock business, and one additional for each partner.

6. Rule the foot lines as shown, and the schedule will be ready to receive the accounts.

The process of showing results is precisely similar in its order, and the results the same as in "closing the Ledger," which has already been so fully explained.

There are many kinds of business statements in use, each possessing some peculiar merit, and all having the same general purpose in view, viz.: that of exhibiting the real and progressive condition of the business represented. The forms hitherto used in this work, and particularly the one on page 121, are both simple and comprehensive, and would possibly be preferred by one not versed in the processes and technicalities of Book-keeping; but we know of no form that compasses so much within such limited space, as that described above. The example, on page 141, will sufficiently indicate the points of excellence, and give the student a model for his emulation. Let him remember that in no one thing does the proficiency of a practical accountant more plainly manifest itself than in the matter of neatness in arrangement and execution. The art of *ruling* tastefully, unimportant as it may seem, is one not easily acquired nor overrated.

EXAMPLES FOR PRACTICE.

THE student is requested to render statements after the form on page 141, from the following materials:

EXAMPLE 1.   TRIAL BALANCE.   *Dr.*   *Cr.*

Stock - - - - - - - - - - - -	881	5000	
Bills Receivable - - - - - - - -	1500	1000	
John Mason - - - - - - - -	300	175	
Cash - - - - - - - - - - -	5794	67	4800
Merchandise - (Amount unsold, $1200)	3500	2759	50
Peter Smith - - - - - - - - -	4000	1500	
Robert Pendergast - - - - - - -		384	
Expense - - - - - - - - - -	875	83	
Bills Payable - - - - - - - -	1500	1750	
Charles Ryan - - - - - - - - -		483	
	17851	50	17851	50

EXAMPLE 2.   TRIAL BALANCE.   *Dr.*   *Cr.*

Stock - - - - - - - - - -	141	78	3000
Merchandise - (Amount unsold, $1000)	5000	3700	
George Hopkins - - - - - - -	1500	953	84
Robert Westcott - - - - - - -	753		
Abram Woodfall - - - - - -	900		
Peter Denyse - - - - - - - -	110	500	
Robert Rantoul - - - - - - -	732	98	500
James Jackson - - - - - - -	75		
E. E. Ellsworth - - - - - - -	500	983	
Cash - - - - - - - - - -	9753	20	8748	90
Expense - - - - - - - - -	450		
Commission - - - - - - - - -		183	22
Bills Receivable - - - - - - -	1700	150	
Bills Payable - - - - - - - -	1500	5000	
Shipment to Detroit - - - - - -	4000	4598	
Edward Rice - - - - - - - -	700	874	
Peter Renwick - - - - - - -	50		
Edwin C. Packard - - - - - -	900	150	
Benj. F. Holmes - - - - - - -	75		
F. R. Perley - - - - - - - -	500		
	29340	96	29340	96

PRACTICAL EXERCISES.

[To be written up after the manner of Set 2.]

TRANSACTIONS.—SECOND SERIES.

Feb. 1.—Commenced business with the following resources and liabilities, taken from the Balance Sheet of previous Ledger.* **Resources:** Cash, $1822.20; Bills Receivable, $171.50; Robert Baker's account, $350; Henry Ivison's do., $222.50; J. C. Bryant's do., $186; L. Fairbanks' do., $293.75; **Liabilities:** our note favor of James Dawes, for $2500 ---- Bo't of Springer & Whiteman, on %, 20 bags Rio Coffee, 1670 lbs., @ 15¢; 15 tierces Rice, 7500 lbs., @ 4¢; 15 hhds. Cuba Sugar, 14000 lbs., @ 5¢.

2.—Bo't of Alex. Cowley, for Cash, 12 hhds. N. O. Molasses, 720 gals., @ 40¢; 20 boxes Soap, 1450 lbs., @ 8¢; 10 brls. Pork, 2000 lbs., @ 10¢.

3.—Sold Lewis Lyman, on %, 30 lbs. Coffee, @ 18¢; 20 do. Rice, @ 5½¢; 100 do. Sugar, @ 6¢ ----- Received Cash of Robert Baker, in full of %, $———.

4.—Paid Cash for stationery and incidental expenses, $20.

5.—Sold Alonzo Mitchell, on %, 1 bag Rio Coffee, 80 lbs., @ 18¢; 20 gals. N. O. Molasses, @ 50¢; 30 lbs. Rice, @ 5½¢ ----- Bo't of Peter Duff, for Cash, 300 lbs. English Dairy Cheese, @ 20¢; 250 lbs. Butter, @ 18¢ ----- Sold John R. Penn, on his note @ 30 ds., 5 boxes Soap, 350 lbs., @ 10¢; 6 bags Rio Coffee, 485 lbs., @ 16¢.

6.—Bo't of S. S. Packard, on our note @ 10 ds., 40 hf. chests Y. H. Tea, 2356 lbs., @ 35¢ ----- Sold Charles Strong, for Cash, 10 hf. chests Tea, 580 lbs., @ 38¢; 100 lbs. English Dairy Cheese, @ 22¢.

9.—Sold Samuel Davis, for Cash, 50 lbs. Butter, @ 20¢; 50 lbs. Coffee, @ 18¢; 30 gals. Molasses, @ 50¢.

10.—Sold Henry Dwight, for Cash, 30 gals. Molasses, @ 50¢; 10 lbs. Rice, @ 6¢; 1 box Soap, 75 lbs., @ 10¢.

12.—Paid clerk's salary in Cash, $15 ----- Bo't of James Simpson, on %, 15 brls. Crushed Sugar, 2520 lbs., @ 10¢.

15.—Rec'd Cash on % of Henry Ivison, $100 ----- Sold Thomas Hunter, on %, 5 hf. chests Tea, 275 lbs., @ 50¢; 50 lbs. English Dairy Cheese, @ 23¢; 25 lbs. Rice, @ 5¢ ----- Sold Henry Ivison, on %, 20 gals. Molasses, @ 50¢; 3 boxes Soap, 210 lbs., @ 10¢.

16.—Rec'd Cash in full of J. C. Bryant's %, $——— ----- Sold W. H. Joeckel, for Cash, 2 brls. Crushed Sugar, 330 lbs., @ 11¢.

17.—Sold Lewis Lyman, on %, 50 lbs. Rio Coffee, @ 20¢; 100 lbs. Crushed Sugar, @ 11¢.

19.—Paid Cash in full, for our note, favor of S. S. Packard, dated Feb. 6, due this day, $824.60.

* See Trial Balance, page 125.

150

20.—Sold Robert Burns, for Cash, 100 lbs. Crushed Sugar, @ 11¢ - - - - -
Received Cash of Henry Ivison, in full of %, $153.50.

22.—Paid James Simpson Cash in full of %, $252 - - - - - Sold Philip
Stone, for Cash, 4 hf. chests Tea, 225 lbs., @ 50¢.

23.—Sold Thomas Hunter, on %, 50 lbs. English Dairy Cheese, @ 25¢ ;
75 do. Crushed Sugar, @ 11¢; 15 do. Coffee, @ 20¢ ; 2 boxes Soap,
140 lbs., @ 10¢.

25.—Sold Alonzo Mitchell, on %, 2 hhds. Cuba Sugar, 1850 lbs., @ 6¢
- - - - - Received Cash in full for J. M. Bradstreet's note of the 3d
ult., due March 5, $96.50 ; also for J. McMillan's note, due Mar. 1,
$75.   Total, $171.50.

27.—Paid Cash for store rent, $100.

STATEMENT.

The student is expected to produce the following results from
the foregoing transactions :

TRIAL BALANCE.

Stock - - - - - - - - - - - -	2500		3045	95
Bills Receivable - - - - - - - -	284	10	174	50
Cash - - - - - - - - - - -	3242	50	1920	60
L. Fairbanks - - - - - - - - -	293	75		
Alonzo Mitchell - - - - - - - -	137	05		
Merchandise (Amount unsold, $2500) - - -	3036	10	961	45
Bills Payable - - - - - - - -	824	60	3324	60
Springer & Whiteman - - - - - -			1250	50
Lewis Lyman - - - - - - - -	33	50		
Expense - - - - - - - - - -	135			
Thos. Hunter - - - - - - - -	188			
	10674	60	10674	60

FINANCIAL STATEMENT.

	Resources.		*Liabilities.*	
Merchandise - - - - - - - - -	2500			
Bills Receivable - - - - - - - -	112	60		
Cash - - - - - - - - - -	1321	90		
L. Fairbanks - - - - - - - - -	293	75		
Alonzo Mitchell - - - - - - - -	137	05		
Bills Payable - - - - - - - -			2500	
Springer & Whiteman - - - - - -			1250	50
Lewis Lyman - - - - - - - -	33	50		
Thos. Hunter - - - - - - - -	188			
Stock (Present Worth) - - - - - - -			836	30
	4586	80	4586	80

QUESTIONS FOR REVIEW.

REMARKS, PAGE 128.

1. In what sense is this a continuation of Set 1?—*2.* What different plan is adopted in the keeping of property accounts?—*3.* When is it customary to keep other than a general Merchandise account?—*4.* When the business commences with a capital, what is the first entry?—*5.* What account is credited with the investment?—*6.* What does Stock account represent?— *7.* What is the technical meaning of the term "Sundries?"—*8.* Why is it used in Journal or Ledger entries?

ORDER AND PURPOSE OF CLOSING THE LEDGER, PAGE 142.

9. In what condition was the Ledger of Set 1 left?—*10.* Under what circumstances is this sufficient?—*11.* When is it necessary to "close" the Ledger accounts?—*12.* When an account is closed, how is the *balance* or *difference* exhibited?—*13.* How many classes of accounts are there in Double Entry?—*14.* What is the distinction?—*15.* What are they called?—*16.* What is meant by FINANCIAL accounts?—*17.* What by BUSINESS?—*18.* What is the object of closing the Ledger?—*19.* Why are the gains and losses in business permitted to appear in the BUSINESS accounts, instead of being carried directly to the proprietor's account?—*20.* How often is it customary to credit the proprietor with his gains?—*21.* To what condition is the Ledger restored when the gains and losses are transferred to the proprietor's account?— *22.* What is the first thing necessary after posting all the entries to the Ledger?—*23.* In what sense is the Trial Balance a test of the correctness of the work?—*24.* What two features are presented by the Trial Balance on page 143?—*25.* How may the *present condition* of a business be shown?—*26.* How are resources shown on the Ledger?—*27.* How liabilities?—*28.* How losses?— *29.* How gains?—*30.* What two accounts may be used to show these results?—*31.* What is contained in the Loss and Gain account?—*32.* What in the Balance account?—*33.* Can you learn from the Merchandise account the value of Merchandise unsold?—*34.* How is it ascertained?—*35.* When the Merchandise account is credited with the inventory of unsold Merchandise, what will the account represent?—*36.* What is the process of *closing* an account?—*37.* In closing an account, why is the *difference* placed on the smaller side?—*38.* What test have we for ascertaining if the balances of the accounts are properly transferred?—*39.* What accounts are contained in the " Second Trial Balance?"—*40.* Why will the difference in the Stock account, after the gain or loss has been transferred, equal the difference in the Balance account when all the resources and liabilities have been entered?—*41.* Is it necessary in closing the Ledger to open a Balance account?—*42.* How may the same effect be produced?—*43.* What is the *first* step in the order of closing?—*44.* Second?—*45.* Third?—*46.* Fourth?—*47.* Fifth?—*48.* Sixth?

SET 3.—DOUBLE ENTRY.

(Corresponding with Set 3, Part 1.)

DAY-BOOK AND JOURNAL COMBINED.

WITH FULL STATEMENTS AND EXPLANATIONS, SHOWING THE DIS-
TINCTIONS BETWEEN DOUBLE AND SINGLE ENTRY.

Business Adverse.

REMARKS.

THE transactions of this set are the same as those in Set 3, Part I., and are selected for the purpose of showing the exact difference between Single Entry and Double Entry. A careful study of the two sets in their similar and dissimilar points will open to the mind of the student a clearer distinction between the two methods of accounts than could be effected in any other way. This distinction is most apparent in the Ledger where it will be seen that the *additional* accounts required by Double Entry relate exclusively to particular speculations, and are useful, mainly, to denote gains and losses.

Another decided improvement in this over the preceding set, relates to the form of the original book of entry, which here combines the Day-Book and Journal. There is no doubt as to the preference of this plan over that of separate books. The only objection that can be arrayed against it is the difficulty sometimes of combining the historical with the journal expression in a manner to preserve the unity of the entry without destroying the individuality of its parts. A little practice, however, will remove this difficulty, and lead the student into a concise and symmetrical form of expression, at once comprehensive and business-like.

It is not deemed necessary to repeat the auxiliary forms of Sales-Book, Cash-Book, and Bill-Book, for the reason that there are no improvements to suggest. Auxiliary books are used for their convenience in classifying the departments of business, and do not pertain necessarily to any particular theory or method of accounts. In Single Entry, however, they are often essential in preserving a sufficient record of resources and liabilities, which in Double Entry are shown independently in the Ledger.

The manner of *closing* the accounts differs from Set 2 only in bringing down the resources and liabilities under the accounts themselves, instead of transferring them to a separate account like " Balance." A few of the accounts, containing only *one* item, are necessarily closed, and the balances brought down. This plan is sometimes adopted in business, for the purpose of exhibiting the condition of affairs on the Ledger *at some certain date.*

The method of showing general results through a detailed statement is commended to the careful attention of the student.

Albany, July 1, 1879.

			DR.	CR.
1	Sundries, To H. B. Bryant,			9075
	For investment, as follows :			
3	Merchandise, As per inventory,		4750	
4	Bills Receivable, " " Bill Book,		1500	
6	Cash, " " Cash Book,		1200	
5	John R. Penn, Balance of %,		500	
7	L. Fairbanks, " "		750	
8	Alonzo Gaston, " "		375	
	"			
2	Sundries, To H. D. Stratton,			8000
	For investment, as follows :			
9	Real Estate, House and lot val. at,		5000	
6	Cash,* Am't in Union Bank,		3000	
	"			
10	Expense,		5	
6	To Cash,			5
	Paid for postage stamps, pens, etc.			
	"			
6	Cash,		39	
3	To Merchandise,			39
	Sold Robt. Van Schaick, per S. B.			
	2			
6	Cash,		250	
5	To John R. Penn,			250
	Received on %.			
	"			
10	Expense,		10	
6	To Cash,			10
	Paid for printing hand-bills.			
			17379	17379

* Some houses keep a regular bank account in their main books, debiting the bank with deposits, and crediting it with checks drawn; while others keep the account only in an auxiliary book, and count the cash in bank the same as that in safe. We have, in this instance, adopted the latter plan.

Albany, July 3, 1879.

		Dr.		Cr.	
11	James Johnson,	192			
3	To Merchandise,			192	
	Per Sales Book.				
	"				
6	Cash,	17	50		
3	To Merchandise,			17	50
	Petty sales, per C. B.				
	4				
4	Bills Receivable,	108	20		
3	To Merchandise,			108	20
	Sold E. H. Bender, per S. B.				
	"				
10	Expense,	175			
6	To Cash,			175	
	Paid C. Jones, repairing store.				
	5				
3	Merchandise, To Sundries,	1359	50		
12	To Claflin, Mellen & Co.,			575	
	Invoice of Boots and Shoes.				
13	" A. T. Stewart & Co.,			757	
	Invoice of Dry Goods.				
6	" Cash,			27	50
	Paid freight on above.				
	7				
14	E. B. Rice,	42	45		
3	To Merchandise,			42	45
	Per Sales Book.				
	"				
6	Cash,	375			
8	To Alonzo Gaston,			375	
	Received in full of %.				
		2269	65	2269	65

Albany, July 7, 1879.

		DR.		CR.	
10	Expense,	25			
6	To Cash,			25	
	Paid clerk hire.				
	——— 8 ———				
6	Cash,	19	82		
3	To Merchandise,			19	82
	Sold W. H. Clark, per S. B.				
	——— " ———				
10	Expense,	15	75		
6	To Cash,			15	75
	Paid expenses to New York.				
	——— 10 ———				
15	Benjamin Payn,	23	41		
3	To Merchandise,			23	41
	Per Sales Book.				
	——— " ———				
6	Cash,	500			
4	To Bills Receivable,			500	
	In full of Robt. Bruce's note.				
	——— " ———				
13	A. T. Stewart & Co.,	300			
6	To Cash,			300	
	Paid them on %.				
	——— " ———				
4	Bills Receivable,	173			
3	To Merchandise,			173	
	Sold C. S. Sill, per S. B.				
		1056	98	1056	98

4

Albany, July 12, 1879.

		Dr.		Cr.	
2	H. D. Stratton,	75			
16	To Bills Payable,			75	
	Accepted draft favor of P. R. Spencer, per B. B.				
	—— " ——				
6	Cash,	33	50		
3	To Merchandise,			33	50
	Received for petty sales, per C. B.				
	—— " ——				
17	Amos Dean,	180			
3	To Merchandise,			180	
	Per Sales Book.				
	—— *13* ——				
12	Claflin, Mellen & Co.,	575			
16	To Bills Payable,			575	
	Our note to balance %.				
	—— *15* ——				
1	H. B. Bryant,	75			
6	To Cash,			75	
	Paid him on %.				
	—— " ——				
6	Cash,	350			
7	To L. Fairbanks,			350	
	Received on %.				
	—— *18* ——				
6	Cash,	252			
3	To Merchandise,			252	
	Sold G. H. Doty, per S. B.				
		1540	50	1540	50

Albany, July 19, 1879.

		DR.			CR.	
10	Expense,	15				
6	To Cash,				15	
	Paid for advertisements in the Evening Journal.					
	20					
18	Victor M. Rice,	82	88			
3	To Merchandise,				82	88
	Per Sales Book.					
	″					
6	Cash,	30				
18	To Victor M. Rice,				30	
	Received on %.					
	″					
10	Expense,	10				
6	To Cash,				10	
	Paid petty expenses per C. B.					
	21					
6	Cash,	50				
17	To Amos Dean,				50	
	Received on %.					
	″					
10	Expense,	183				
6	To Cash,				183	
	Bill of carpenter work, $175; drayage, $5; porterage, $3.					
	22					
4	Bills Receivable,	339				
3	To Merchandise,				339	
	Sold J. R. Morgan, per S. B.					
		709	88		709	88

Albany, July 23, 1879.

DR.　　　CR.

19 3	James Sheldon, To Merchandise, Per Sales Book.	132	24			132	24
6 3	Cash, To Merchandise, Sold R. Metcalf, per S. B.	234				234	
6 3	Cash, To Merchandise, Sold Chas. Heydon, per S. B.	106				106	
6 14	Cash, To E. B. Rice, Received in full of %.	42	45			42	45
20 3	William Shepard, To Merchandise, Per Sales Book.	37	55			37	55
6 3	Cash, To Merchandise, Sold Robt. Dawes, per S. B.	163	20			163	20
16 6	Bills Payable, To Cash, Paid on Accept. favor H. D. S.	75				75	
10 6	Expense, To Cash, Paid clerk hire.	25				25	
		815	44			815	44

24

25

Albany, July 26, 1879.

		DR.			CR.	
21	John Belden,	216	50			
3	To Merchandise,				216	50
	Per Sales Book.					
	''					
13	A. T. Stewart & Co.,	457				
6	To Cash,				457	
	Paid them in full of %.					
	27					
6	Cash,	138	72			
3	To Merchandise,				138	72
	Sold J. H. Lansley, per S. B.					
	29					
6	Cash,	154				
3	To Merchandise,				154	
	Sold W. H. Fiquet, per S. B.					
	''					
6	Cash,	250				
5	To John R. Penn,				250	
	Received in full of %.					
	30					
3	Sundries, To Merchandise,				182	40
	Sold Chas. A. Seeley, per S. B.					
6	Cash, Amount received,	75				
22	Chas. A. Seeley, Balance on %,	107	40			
		1398	62		1398	62

1

Dr.   H. B. Bryant.   Cr.

1879						1879					
July	15	To Cash,	4	75		July	1	By Sundries,	1	9075	
	31	Loss & Gain,	L23	352	94						
	"	*Balance,*	L1	8647	06						
				9075	00					9075	
						Aug.	1	By Balance,	L1	8647	06

2

Dr.   H. D. Stratton.   Cr.

1879						1879					
July	12	To Bills Payable,	4	75		July	1	By Sundries,	1	8000	
	31	Loss & Gain,	L6	352	94						
	31	*Balance,*	L2	7572	06						
				8000	00					8000	
						Aug.	1	By Balance,	L2	7572	06

3

Dr.   Merchandise.   Cr.

1879						1879					
July	1	To H. B. Bryant,	1	4750		July	1	By Cash,	1	39	
	5	Sundries,	2	1359	50		3	J. Johnson,	2	192	
							"	Cash,	"	17	50
							4	Bills Rec'ble,	"	108	20
							7	E. B. Rice,	"	42	45
							8	Cash,	3	19	82
							10	Benj. Payn,	"	23	41
							12	Bills Rec'ble,	"	173	
							"	Cash,	4	33	50
							13	Amos Dean,	"	180	
							13	Cash,	"	252	
							20	Vict. M. Rice,	5	82	88
							22	Bills Rec'ble,	"	339	
							23	Jas. Shelden,	6	132	21
							"	Cash,	"	234	
							24	"	"	106	
							25	W. Shepard,	"	37	55
							"	Cash,	"	163	20
							26	John Belden,	7	216	50
							27	Cash,	"	138	72
							29	"	"	154	
							30	Sundries,	"	182	40
							31	*Balance,*	L3	3000	
							"	*Loss & Gain,*	L23	242	13
				6109	50					6109	50
Aug.	1	To Balance,	L3	3000							

4

Dr.   Bills Receivable.   Cr.

1879						1879					
July	1	To H. B. Bryant,	1	1500		July	10	By Cash,	3	500	
	4	Mdse.,	2	108	20		31	*Balance*,	14	*1620*	*20*
	12	"	3	173							
	22	"	5	339							
				2120	20					2120	20
Aug.	1	To Balance,	14	1620	20						

5

Dr.   John R. Penn.   Cr.

1879					1879				
July	1	To H. B. Bryant,	1	500	July	2	By Cash,	1	250
						29	"	7	250
				500					500

6

Dr.   Cash.   Cr.

1879						1879					
July	1	To H. B. Bryant,	1	1200		July	1	By Expense,	1	5	
	"	H.D. Stratton,	"	3000			2	"	"	10	
	"	Mdse.,	"	39			4	"	2	175	
	2	J. R. Penn,	"	250			5	Mdse.,	"	27	50
	3	Mdse.,	2	17	50		7	Expense,	3	25	
	7	A. Gaston,	"	375			8	"	"	15	75
	8	Mdse.,	3	19	82		10	A.T.Stw.&Co.	"	300	
	10	Bills Rec'ble,	"	500			15	H. B. Bryant,	4	75	
	12	Mdse.,	4	33	50		19	Expense,	5	15	
	16	L. Fairbanks,	"	350			20	"	"	10	
	18	Mdse.,	"	252			21	"	"	183	
	20	V. M. Rice,	5	30			25	Bills Payable,	6	75	
	21	Amos Dean,	"	50			"	Expense,	"	25	
	23	Mdse.,	6	234			26	A.T.Stw.&Co.	7	457	
	24	"	"	106			31	*By Balance*,	16	*5881*	*94*
	"	E. B. Rice,	"	42	45						
	25	Mdse.,	"	163	20						
	27	"	7	138	72						
	29	"	"	154							
	"	J. R. Penn,	"	250							
	30	Mdse.,	"	75							
				7280	19					7280	19
Aug.	1	To Balance,	16	5881	94						

7

| Dr. | | | | | L. Fairbanks. | | | | Cr |

1879						1879				
July	1	To H. B. Bryant,	1	750		July	16	By Cash,	4	350
							31	*Balance,*	L7	*400*
				750	*					750
Aug.	1	To Balance,	L7	400						

8

| Dr. | | | | | Alonzo Gaston. | | | | Cr. |

1879						1879				
July	1	To H. B. Bryant,	1	375		July	7	By Cash,	2	375

9

| Dr. | | | | | Real Estate. | | | | Cr. |

1879						1879				
July	1	To H.D.Stratton,	1	5000		July	31	*By Balance,*	L9	*5000*
Aug.	1	To Balance,	L9	5000						

10

| Dr. | | | | | Expense. | | | | | Cr. |

1879							1879					
July	1	To Cash,	1	5			July	31	*By Loss & Gain,*	L23	*463*	*75*
	2	"	"	10								
	4	"	2	175								
	7	"	3	25								
	8	"	"	15	75							
	19	"	5	15								
	20	"	"	10								
	21	"	"	183								
	25	"	6	25								
				463	75						463	75

11

Dr. James Johnson. *Cr.*

1879						1879				
July	3	To Mdse.,	2	192		July	31	*By Balance,*	L11	*192*
Aug.	1	To Balance,	L11	192						

12

Dr. Claflin, Mellen & Co. *Cr.*

1879						1879				
July	15	To Bills Payable,	4	575		July	5	By Mdse.,	2	575

13

Dr. A. T. Stewart & Co. *Cr.*

1879						1879				
July	10	To Cash,	3	300		July	5	By Mdse.,	2	757
"	26	" "	7	457						
				757						757

14

Dr. E. B. Rice. *Cr.*

1879							1879					
July	7	To Mdse.	2	42	45		July	24	By Cash,	6	42	45

15

Dr. Benjamin Payn. *Cr.*

1879							1879					
July	10	To Mdse.,	3	23	41		July	31	*By Balance,*	L15	*23*	*41*
Aug.	1	To Balance,	1.15	23	41							

16

| Dr. | | | | | | | | Bills Payable. | | | Cr. |

1879						1879					
July	25	To Cash,	6	75		July	12	By H.D. Stratton,	4	75	
"	31	*Balance,*	L16	*575*			15	Claf. M. & Co.	"	575	
				650						650	
						Aug.	1	By Balance,	L16	575	

17

| Dr. | | | | | | | | Amos Dean. | | | Cr. |

1879						1879					
July	13	To Mdse.,	4	180		July	21	By Cash,	5	50	
							31	*Balance,*	L17	*130*	
				180						180	
Aug.	1	To Balance,	L17	130							

18

| Dr. | | | | | | | | Victor M. Rice. | | | Cr. |

1879							1879						
July	20	To Mdse.,	5	82	88		July	20	By Cash,	5	30	
								31	*Balance,*	L18	*52*	*83*
				82	88						82	88
Aug.	1	To Balance,	L18	52								

19

| Dr. | | | | | | | | James Sheldon. | | | Cr. |

1879							1879						
July	23	To Mdse.,	6	132	24		July	31	*By Balance,*	L19	*132*	*24*
Aug.	1	To Balance,	L19	132	24							

20

| Dr. | | | | | | | | William Shepard. | | | Cr. |

1879							1879						
July	25	To Mdse.,	6	37	55		July	31	*By Balance,*	L20	*37*	*55*
Aug.	1	To Balance,	L20	37	55							

21

Dr.   John Belden.   Cr.

1879						1879					
July	26	To Mdse.,	7	216	50	July	31	By Balance,	L21	216	50
Aug.	1	To Balance,	L21	216	50						

22

Dr.   Chas. A. Seeley.   Cr.

1879						1879					
July	30	To Mdse.,	7	107	40	July	31	By Balance,	L22	107	40
Aug.	1	To Balance,	L22	107	40						

23

Dr.   Loss and Gain.   Cr.

1879						1879					
July	31	To Mdse.,	L3	242	13	July	31	By H. B. Bryant,	L1	352	94
	"	Expense,	L10	463	75		"	H. D. Stratton,	L2	352	94
				705	88					705	88

167

STATEMENT.

THE following detailed statement should be carefully compared with the Single Entry Statement on page 67, that the characteristic features of the two systems may be thoroughly appreciated. We have designated the proper classification of accounts in the Trial Balance and have included *all* the Ledger accounts, that the general footings may be made to agree with the footings of the Journal In rendering the Statement, those accounts which cancel or balance, are, of course, omitted. With this form of Trial Balance it would scarcely be necessary to do more than carry the *balances* of the accounts into the statement columns as in the Statement on page 121; but this form gives the philosophy more in detail.

			TRIAL BALANCE.		Total Footings.				Balances.		
				Dr.		Cr.		Dr.		Cr.	
1	H. B. Bryant,	Financial - - -		75		9075				9000	
2	H. D. Stratton,	Financial - - -		75		8000				7925	
3	Merchandise,	Business - - -		6109	50	2867	37	3242	13		
4	Bills Receivable,	Financial - - -		2120	20	500		1620	20		
5	John R. Penn,	Financial - - -		500		500					
6	Cash,	Financial - - -		7280	19	1398	25	5881	94		
7	L. Fairbanks,	Financial - - -		750		350		400			
8	Alonzo Gaston,	Financial - - -		375		375					
9	Real Estate,	Business - -		5000				5000			
10	Expense,	Business - - -		463	75			463	75		
11	James Johnson,	Financial - - -		192				192			
12	Claf., Mellen & Co.,	Financial - - -		575		575					
13	A. T. Stewart,	Financial - - -		757		757					
14	E. B. Rice,	Financial - - -		42	45	42	45				
15	Benjamin Payn,	Financial - - -		23	41			23	41		
16	Bills Payable,	Financial - - -		75		650				575	
17	Amos Dean,	Financial - - -		180		50		130			
18	Victor M. Rice,	Financial - - -		82	88	30		52	88		
19	James Sheldon,	Financial - - -		132	24			132	24		
20	William Shepard,	Financial - - -		37	55			37	55		
21	John Belden,	Financial - - -		216	50			216	50		
22	Chas. A. Seelcy,	Financial - - -		107	40			107	40		
				25170	07	25170	07	17500	00	17500	00

_____ INVENTORY. _____

Mdse. unsold - - - - - - - - - - - - - - - $3000
Real Estate - - - - - - - - - - - - - - - - 5000

LOSSES AND GAINS.—BUSINESS ACCOUNTS.

				Losses.		Gains.	
3	MERCHANDISE	Outlay	$6109 50				
		Returns, . $2867 37					
		Value unsold, 3000 00	5867 37				
		Net loss		242	13		
10	EXPENSE	Outlay for Expenses		463	75		
		TOTAL NET LOSS				705	88
		H. B. B's ½ net loss $352 94		705	88	705	88
		H. D. S's " " . . 352 94					

RESOURCES AND LIABILITIES.—FINANCIAL ACCOUNTS.

				Resources.		Liabilities.	
	1.—From Inventories of unsold property.						
	MERCHANDISE			3000			
	REAL ESTATE			5000			
	2.—From Ledger Accounts.						
4	BILLS RECEIVABLE,	Others' notes received,	$2120 20				
		" " disp. of,	500 00				
		" " on hand	. . . .	1620	20		
6	CASH	Amount received . .	$7280 19				
		" paid out . .	1398 25				
		" on hand . .	. . . .	5881	94		
7	L. FAIRBANKS . . .	Our % against him	$750 00				
		His " " us .	350 00				
		He owes us		400			
11	JAMES JOHNSON . .	He owes us		192			
15	BENJ. PAYN . . .	" " "		23	41		
16	BILLS PAYABLE . .	Our notes issued .	$650 00				
		" " redeemed .	75 00				
		" " outstanding	. . . .			575	
17	AMOS DEAN	Our % against him .	$180 00				
		His " " us .	50 00				
		He owes us		130			
18	VICTOR M. RICE . .	Our % against him .	$32 88				
		His " " us .	30 00				
		He owes us		52	88		
19	JAMES SHELDON . .	" " "		132	24		
20	WILLIAM SHEPARD .	" " "		37	55		
21	JOHN BELDEN . . .	" " "		216	50		
22	CHAS. A. SEELEY .	" " "		107	40		
1	H. B. BRYANT . . .	His net investment . .	$9000 00				
		" " loss	352 94				
		HIS PRESENT INTEREST				8647	06
2	H. D. STRATTON . .	His net investment . .	$7925 00				
		" " loss	352 94				
		HIS PRESENT INTEREST				7572	06
				16794	12	16794	12

EXAMPLES FOR PRACTICE.

THE following examples are to be rendered in the form of the Statement on page 169.

EXAMPLE 1.   TRIAL BALANCE.   *Dr.*   *Cr.*

	Dr.		Cr.	
Warren P. Spencer, (Partner) - - - -	700		5724	58
J. C. Bryant, do. - - - -			5024	58
Merchandise (Amount unsold, $5000) - - -	12000		7594	
Cash - - - - - - - - - - - - -	15752	25	9692	84
Bills Receivable - - - - - - - - -	4000		1500	
Bills Payable - - - - - - - - - -	9000		12000	
E. G. Folsom - - - - - - - - - -	750			
E. R. Felton - - - - - - - - - -	123	75	965	
Expense - - - - - - - - - - -	175			
	42501	00	42501	00

EXAMPLE 2.   TRIAL BALANCE.   *Dr.*   *Cr.*

	Dr.		Cr.	
James W. Lusk, (Partner) - - - - - -			4500	
H. W. Ellsworth, do. - - - -	398	72	5000	
H. C. Spencer, do. - - - -			4500	
Cash - - - - - - - - -	17594	28	15329	50
Bills Receivable - - - - - - - -	7500		4300	
Merchandise, (Inventory, $1000) - - -	6794		5382	50
Real Estate, (do. 5000) - - -	5000		125	
Expense - - - - - - - - - -	150			
Bills Payable - - - - - - - - -	4000		5700	
Robert Paton - - - - - - - - -	2000			
Samuel Ogden - - - - - - - -	1400			
	44837	00	44837	00

QUESTIONS FOR REVIEW.

REMARKS, PAGE 154.

1. What is the purpose of Set 3 ?—*2.* With what previous set does it correspond ?—*3.* Where is the distinction between Single and Double Entry most apparent ?—*4.* To what do the *additional* accounts in Double Entry relate ?—*5.* For what are they useful ?—*6.* What improvement has this set over Set 2 ? —*7.* What is the objection usually urged against combining the Day-Book and Journal ?—*8.* What is the general purpose of auxiliary books ?—*9.* For what are they used in Single Entry ?—*10.* In what does the method of closing the accounts in this Ledger differ from the preceding ?—Is it usual to *bring down* single items in the Ledger ?—*12.* When is this proper ?

NOTE.—Let this set be followed by the "Exercises" on page 69.

Set 4.—Double Entry.

GENTLEMEN'S FURNISHING BUSINESS.

(PARTNERSHIP.)

JOURNAL, CASH-BOOK, AND SALES-BOOK, USED AS PRINCIPAL BOOKS.

Business Prosperous.

REMARKS.

THE characteristic feature of this set consists in the peculiar arrangement and use of the original books of entry. Hitherto the transactions, whatever auxiliary books have been used, have all been entered in the Journal, and from thence posted to the Ledger. This plan, although having some advantages, is objectionable upon the ground of too much labor, nearly all the transactions being entered twice or more before being carried to the Ledger.

The plan of posting directly from the original books of entry, such as the Cash-Book, Sales-Book, etc., is not only practical and business-like, but serves, in the most striking manner to enforce the theory of the science, and to disarm that class of objectionists who insist that Double Entry requires vastly more writing than Single Entry.

The only difficulty in the way of posting directly from the original books lies in the danger of conflicting the entries, or posting the same amounts *twice*. For instance, the debit side of the Cash-Book comprises in itself a double entry, which is equivalent to the Journal entry " Cash, Dr. To Sundries." In posting from the Cash-Book, the total of the *debit* side is carried to the Cash account in the Ledger, and the item comprising that amount to the *credit* side of the various accounts mentioned, among which is Merchandise. It is very evident that if all the Merchandise sold be credited from the Sales-Book, the amount sold for Cash would be credited *twice ;* hence the necessity of an extra column in the Sales-Book for Cash sales which are omitted in posting from the Sales-Book. The special " Mdse." and " Expense" columns in the Cash-Book are to save the necessity of so many special entries to these accounts in the Ledger. The method of posting from the Cash and Sales-Books is extremely simple. The amounts in the " General" column of the Cash-Book may be posted at any time—the page of the Ledger being indicated in a column provided for that purpose, the " Mdse." and " Expense " columns at the end of the month, or as often as may be best to close the Cash-Book. The sales for Cash are checked off in the Sales-Book, and the amounts extended into the " Cash " column. The other accounts from the Sales-Book may be posted at any time, the page of the Ledger being indicated in the proper column. The sales for notes are marked *inside* the margin, " B. R." and, of course, posted to Bills Receivable account. Instead of indicating the page from which the transactions are posted, the initials of the original book are given in the Ledger.

Chicago, September 1, 1878.

		DR.	CR.
7	Merchandise,	6750	
2	To John R. Penn,		6750
	Amount invested, per inventory.		
	"		
2	John R. Penn,	1750	
14	To Bills Payable,		1750
	Assumed for him.		
	"		
3	Sundries, To J. C. Bryant,		5900
	Amounts invested.		
4	Bills Receivable, J. Smith's note, $750		
	H. Young's " 750	1500	
5	J. T. Calkins, Balance of %.	500	
8	E. R. Felton, " "	376	
9	J. H. Goldsmith, " "	1170	
10	Jas. Atwater, " "	1250	
11	P. C. Schuyler, " "	1104	
	"		
3	J. C. Bryant, To Sundries,	900	
	Liabilities assumed.		
12	To Chas. Taylor, Balance of %.		500
13	J. W. Lusk, " "		400
	15		
13	J. W. Lusk,	400	
14	To Bills Payable,		400
	Our note @ 30 ds. to bal. %.		
	20		
4	Bills Receivable,	1104	
11	To P. C. Schuyler,		1104
	His note @ 60 ds. to bal. %.		
		16804	16804

—————— Cash. ——————

1878						Dr.			
						General.		*Mdse.*	
Sept.	1	S. S. Packard, . .	Amount invested, . . .	1	5000				
	"	Mdse., ...	T. W. W. Sales Book, . .	√			363	72	
	"	Mdse., ...	Petty sales. P. C. B., . .	√			54	25	
	2	J. T. Calkins, . .	On %, ...	5	200				
	3	Mdse., ...	D. V. B. Sales Book, . .	√			89		
	"	Mdse., ...	Petty sales. P. C. B., . .	√			28	90	
	5	Mdse., ...	" " " . .	√			105		
	7	Mdse., ...	J. A. Sales Book, . . .	√			737	50	
	10	James Atwater, .	On %, ...	10	750				
	12	Mdse., ...	Petty sales. P. C. B., . .	√			58		
	14	Mdse., ...	" " " . .	√			138		
	15	Mdse., ...	W. B. Sales Book, . . .	√			128	25	
	16	J. T. Calkins, . .	On %, ...	5	150				
	17	Bills Receivable,	J. Smith's note, ...	4	750				
	"	Interest, ...	On same, ...	15	34	25			
	18	Mdse., ...	Petty sales. P. C. B., . .	√			94	83	
	22	J. H. Goldsmith,	On %, ...	9	1000				
	"	Mdse., ...	Petty sales. P. C. B., . .	√			112	44	
	25	E. R. Felton, . .	In full, ...	8	876				
	"	Mdse., ...	Petty sales. P. C. B., . .	√			83	75	
	26	Mdse., ...	" " " . .	√			58	94	
	"	J. H. Goldsmith,	On %, ...	9	170				
	27	Mdse., ...	Petty sales. P. C. B., . .	√			117	50	
	"	James Atwater, .	On %, ...	10	500				
	28	Mdse., ...	R. McG. Sales Book, . .	√			156	75	
	"	Mdse., ...	Petty sales. P. C. B., . .	√			87	50	
	29	Mdse., ...	" " " . .	√			112	94	
	"	Bills Receivable,	H. Young's note, ...	4	750				
		Interest, ...	On same, ...	15	14	50			
	30	Mdse., ...	Petty sales. P. C. B., . .	√			175		
		MERCHANDISE, *Cr.*, ...		7	2702	27	2702	27	
		CASH, *Dr.*, ...		6	12397	02			

CASH - BOOK.

_____ Cash. _____

1878						Cr.		
						General		*Expense.*
Sept.	1	Expense, ...	Postage stamps, ...	√				3
	2	Charles Taylor, .	On %, ...	12	300			
	4	Expense, ...	2 tons Coal, @ $5, . . .	√				10
	6	Expense, ...	Bill of Stationery, . . .	√				15
	"	Expense, ...	Hands, for shop-work, .	√				150
	7	Mdse., ...	Invoice Cloths. J. B , . .	7	3000			
	10	Expense, ...	Gas bill, ...	√				15
	13	Expense, ...	Hands, for shop-work, .	√				175
	15	Bills Payable, . .	Our note, favor H. B., . .	14	1000			
	"	Interest, ...	On same, ...	15	46	75		
	18	Expense, ...	Clerks' Salaries, ...	√				112
	20	Expense, ...	Hands, for shop-work, .	√				250
	25	Expense, ...	Rent to September 30, .	√				100
	26	Expense, ...	Porterage and Drayage, .	√				35
	23	Expense, ...	Hands, for shop-work, .	√				275
	30	Expense, ...	Partners' salaries to date,	√				606
		EXPENSE, *Dr.*, ...		16	1746			1746
		CASH, *Cr.*, ...		6	6092	75		
		Balance on hand, ...			6304	27		
					12397	02		

1

Chicago, September 1, 1878.

						General.		Cash.	

THERON W. WOOLSON,   *Mt. Pleasant, Ia.*

4 doz. Shirts, 2d quality,	48 @ $1 00	$48 00					
6 " Union Neckties,	72 " 38¢	27 36					
20 " Linen Hdkfs,	240 " 50¢	120 00					
3 pcs. Cassimere,	150 yds., " 1 25	187 50					
		$382 86					
Disc. off, 5%,		19 14	√			363	72

——— " ———

IRA PACKARD,   *Peru, Ind.*

50 Boys' Overcoats,	@ $5 50	$275 00				
50 " "	" 7 50	375 00	4	650	
B. R. *Note @ 6 mo.*					

——— *3* ———

D. V. BELL,   *Chicago.*

1 Dress Suit for self,		$50 00			
1 Overcoat for son,		15 00			
1 box Hdkfs.,	6 doz. @ $4 00	24 00	√		89

——— *5* ———

J. H. GOLDSMITH,   *Detroit.*

2 pcs. Eng. Broadcloth, 100 yds. @ $4 00	$400 00				
50 Military Coats, per order, " 13 00	500 00	9	900	

——— *7* ———

JAMES ALLEN,   *Dubuque.*

20 Zouave Uniforms,	@ $25 00	$500 00			
1 pc. Striped Satin,	50 yds., " 5 00	250 00			
		$750 00			
Disc. off Satin, @ 5%,		12 50	√		737	50

——— *12* ———

JAMES ATWATER,   *Madison.*

1 lot Ready-made Clothing, viz.:					
10 Coats,	@ $3 00	$30 00			
20 "	" 3 50	70 00			
50 "	" 5 00	250 00			
8 pair Pants,	" 3 00	24 00			
25 " "	" 4 00	100 00			
50 Vests,	" 1 50	75 00			
25 "	" 3 00	75 00			
1 Overcoat,		15 00	19	639	
				2189		1190	22

Chicago, September 15, 1878.

					General.		Cash.	
Amounts forward,					2189		1190	22
WILLIAM BAKER,			*Springfi.ld.*					
5 doz. Cravats,	60 @	75¢	$45 00					
3 " "	36 "	$1 00	36 00					
9 " Linen Hdkfs.,	108 "	50¢	54 00					
			$135 00					
Disc. off, 5%,			6 75	√			128	25
—— *17* ——								
J. T. CALKINS,			*North Bend, Ind.*					
50 Military Coats (privates), @	$10 00		$500 00					
5 " " (officers),	" 15 00		75 00	5	575			
—— *18* ——								
C. D. BRAGDON,			*Rock Island.*					
50 ready-made Coats,	@ $5 00		$250 00					
100 prs. Pants,	" 3 00		300 00					
50 doz. Collars,	" 1 50		75 00					
5 " F. Y. Shirts,	60 " 1 75		105 00	4	730			
B. R. *Note @ 6 mos.*								
—— *20* ——								
GEORGE E. HARVEY,			*Green Bay.*					
100 Zouave Uniforms,	@ $20 00		$2000 00					
50 Military Coats, "Co. H."	" 10 00		500 00	4	2500			
B. R. *Note @ 60 ds.*								
—— *25* ——								
JAMES W. LUSK,			*Chicago.*					
50 Uniforms ("Linc. Green") @	$25 00		$1250 00					
30 " (Zouaves)	" 15 00		450 00	13	1700			
—— *28* ——								
ROBERT McGRATH,			*White Pigeon.*					
20 ready-made Boy's Coats,	@ $5 00		$100 00					
30 " " Vests,	" 1 50		45 00					
20 doz. Collars,	" 1 00		20 00					
			$165 00					
Disc. off, 5%,			8 25	√			156	75
—— *30* ——								
E. R. FELTON,			*Peoria.*					
75 Complete Uniforms,	@ $25 00			8	1875			
Sales on time, to credit of Mdse.,				7	9569			
Sales for Cash, posted from C. B.,					1475	22	1475	22
Petty Sales, entered alone on Cash Book,					1227	05		
Total Mdse. sold,					12271	27		

1

Dr. | S. S. Packard. | Cr.

					1878				
					Sept.	1	By Cash,	CB	5000

2

Dr. | John R. Penn. | Cr.

1878					1878				
Sept.	1	To Bills Payable,	J	1750	Sept.	1	By Mdse.,	J	6750

3

Dr. | J. C. Bryant. | Cr.

1878					1878				
Sept.	1	To Sundries,	J	900	Sept.	1	By Sundries,	J	5900

4

Dr. | Bills Receivable. | Cr.

1878					1878				
Sept.	1	To J. C. Bryant,	J	1500	Sept.	17	By Cash,	CB	750
	20	P. C. Schuyler,	J	1104		29	"	CB	750
	1	Mdse.,	SB	650					
	18	"	SB	730					
	20	"	SB	2500					

5

Dr. | J. T. Calkins. | Cr.

1878					1878				
Sept.	1	To J. C. Bryant,	J	500	Sept.	2	By Cash,	CB	200
	15	Mdse.,	SB	575		16	"	CB	150

6

Dr.						Cash.				Cr.
1878 Sept.	30	To Sundries,	CB	12397	02	1878 Sept.	30	By Sundries,	CB	6092	75

7

Dr.						Merchandise.				Cr.
1878 Sept.	1	To J. R. Penn,	J	6750		1878 Sept.	30	By Cash,	CB	2702	27
	7	Cash,	CB	3000			"	Sundries,	SB	9569	

8

Dr.					E. R. Felton.				Cr.
1878 Sept.	1	To J. C. Bryant,	J	376	1878 Sept.	25	By Cash,	CB	376
	30	Mdse.,	SB	1875					

9

Dr.					J. H. Goldsmith.				Cr.
1878 Sept.	1	To J. C. Bryant,	J	1170	1878 Sept.	22	By Cash,	CB	1000
	5	Mdse.,	SB	900		26	"	CB	170

10

Dr.					James Atwater.				Cr.
1878 Sept.	1	To J. C. Bryant,	J	1250	1878 Sept.	10	By Cash,	CB	750
	12	Mdse.,	SB	639		27	"	CB	500

179

11

Dr.   P. C. Schuyler.   Cr.

1878						1878					
Sept.	1	To J. C. Bryant,	J	1104		Sept.	20	By Bills Rec'ble,	J	1104	

12

Dr.   Charles Taylor.   Cr.

1878						1878					
Sept.	2	To Cash,	CB	300		Sept.	1	By J. C. Bryant,	J	500	

13

Dr.   James W. Lusk.   Cr.

1878						1878					
Sept.	15	To Bills Payable,	J	400		Sept.	1	By J. C. Bryant,	J	400	
	25	Mdse.,	SB	1700							

14

Dr.   Bills Payable.   Cr.

1878						1878					
Sept.	15	To Cash,	CB	1000		Sept.	1	By J. R. Penn,	J	1750	
							15	J. W. Lusk,	J	400	

15

Dr.   Interest.   Cr.

1878							1878					
Sept.	15	To Cash,	CB	46	75		Sept.	17	By Cash,	CB	34	25
								29	"	CB	14	50

16

Dr.   Expense.   Cr.

1878										
Sept.	30	To Cash,	CB	1746						

PRACTICAL EXERCISES.

[CONTINUATION OF SET 4.]

TRANSACTIONS.—FOURTH SERIES.

The following routine is a continuation of the business of Set 4, and the transactions should be entered in the proper books and posted in accordance with the plan and instructions of the set, using the same books, and producing at the close a general result of the whole business. As this set is by far the most practical in the treatise, its peculiar points should be thoroughly impressed upon the mind. The student should exercise much care in the symmetrical arrangement of the original books of entry. The accompanying initials will indicate the books to be written up, and their order.

Oct. 1.—Bo't of Dunham & Brokaw, on %, Invoice of Mdse. amounting to $6000, (J.). Sold James Johnson, Freeport, for Cash, 1 doz. Fancy Neckties, @ $1 each; 12 doz. prs. Lisle Thread Stockings, @ $3 per doz. (S. B., C. B.).

2.—Paid shop-hands, Cash, $300 (C. B.)------ Received Cash for petty sales, $119 (C. B.).

3.—Received Cash of J. H. Goldsmith, in full of %, $900 (C. B.)------ Sold E. R. Felton, on %, 6 doz. French Yoke Shirts, @ $18 per doz.; 10 doz. Knit Undershirts, @ $7 per doz.; 8 doz. prs. Knit Drawers, @ $8 per doz. (S. B.).

5.—Received Cash for petty sales, $120 (C. B.)------ Sold Robert Harmer, Vandalia, for Cash, 15 Summer Coats, @ $2; 20 Summer Vests, @ $1.50; 6 doz. Cut-throat Collars, @ $2 per doz. (C. B.).

7.—Paid Cash for repairing store, $150 (C. B.)----- Received Cash for petty sales, $94.83 (C. B.).

8.—Received Cash of J. T. Calkins, in full of %, $725 (C. B.)---- Sold Jacob Horn, Milwaukee, on his note @ 60 ds., 50 Complete Uniforms, @ $20 (S. B.)---- Received Cash for petty sales, $110 (C. B.).

9.—Paid shop-hands, Cash, $297 (C. B.)----- Sold J. W. Lusk, on %, 24 Ready-made Coats, @ $5; 15 prs. Pants, @ $3.75; 30 Vests, @ $2; 1 Fine Overcoat, $25 (S. B.).

10.—Received Cash for petty sales, $119.50 (C. B.).

12.—Received Cash in full for P. C. Schuyler's note, $1104 (C. B.).

15.—Sold Abraham Jackson for Cash, 5 doz. Byron Collars, @ $2 per doz.; 4 doz. D'Orsay Cravats, @ $12 per doz. (S. B., C. B.) - - - - Received Cash for petty sales. $157.30 (C. B.).

16.—Paid Dunham & Brokaw, Cash on %, $3000 (C. B.) - - - - - - Paid shop-hands, Cash, $263 (C. B.) - - - - - Received Cash for petty sales, $85.90 (C. B.).

18.—Sold E. R. Felton, on %, 1 case Overalls, 6 doz. prs., @ $6 per doz.; 2 cases Summer Frocks, 12 doz., @ $18 per doz. (S. B.) - - - - - Received Cash for petty sales, $115 (C. B.).

20.—Received Cash of E. R. Felton, on %, $1500 (C. B.) - - - - - Sold Robert C. Spencer, St. Louis, for Cash, 10 Military Coats, @ $15 ; 5 do. (officers'), @ $25 (S. B., C. B.) - - - - - Received Cash for petty sales, $143 (C. B.).

21.—Paid Cash for salaries, $117 (C. B.) - - - - - Sold Chas. Taylor, on %, 1 piece French Cassimere, 50 yds., @ $3 (S. B.) - - - - - Received Cash for petty sales, $125 (C. B.) - - - - - Paid Dunham & Brokaw, Cash in full of %, $3000 (C. B.).

23.—Paid Shop-hands, Cash, $375 (C. B.) - - - - - Received Cash for petty sales, $75 (C. B.).

25.—Sold James Atwater, on %, 12 Boys' Frocks, @ $2 ; 36 do., @ $5 (S. B.) - - - - - Received Cash for petty sales, $85.90 (C. B.).

27.—Received Cash of James Atwater, in full of %, $843 (C. B.).

28.—Paid Cash for gas bill, $15 ; Rent, $100 (C. B.).

30.—Paid shop-hands, Cash, $400 (C. B.).

INVENTORY : Merchandise unsold, $3000.

STATEMENT.

The above transactions, properly entered, will produce the following result·

	FACE OF LEDGER.				BALANCES.			
	Dr.		Cr.		Dr.		Cr.	
S. S. Packard - - - - - -			5000				5000	
J. R. Penn - - - - - -	1750		6750				5000	
J. C. Bryant - - - - - -	900		5900				5000	
Bills Receivable - - - - -	7484		2604		4880			
Cash - - - - - - -	19272	45	14109	75	5162	70		
Merchandise - - - - - -	15750		16183	95			433	95
E. R. Felton - - - - - -	2745		1876		869			
Charles Taylor - - - - - -	450		500				50	
J. W. Lusk - - - - - -	2361	25	400		1961	25		
Bills Payable - - - - - -	1000		2150				1150	
Interest - - - - - -	46	75	48	75			2	
Expense - - - - - -	3763				3763			
	55522	45	55522	45	16635	95	16635	95

APPENDIX.

HEREIN are given, in their order, the transactions which make up the material of the written sets, in both parts of the book; as also matter for short practical sets which may be profitably used in connection with, and at such points in the student's progress as the teacher may think best.

PART I.—SET I.

New York, July 1, 1879.—Sold Robert Simpson, on %, 10 lbs. Rio Coffee, @ 12¢ ; 1 lb. Best Black Tea, $1 ; 25 lbs. Crushed Sugar, @ 12¢ - - - - - Sold James Cruikshank, on %, 1 box Raisins, 25 lbs., @ 20¢ - - - - - Sold Horace Webster, on %, 1 gal. Vinegar, 75¢ ; 3 lbs. Black Tea, @ 75¢ ; 4 bush. Apples, @ $1.

2.—Sold W. L. Carpenter, on %, 50 lbs. Ham, @ 11¢ ; 1 box Herrings, $2 - - - - - Rec'd cash, on %, $5.

3.—Sold John Shields, on %, 1 brl. Flour, $8 - - - - - Sold Peter Van Wyck, on %, 5 gals. Cider Vinegar, @ 75¢ ; 3 bush. Potatoes, @ $1.

5.—Sold Peter Cooper, on %, 6 gals. Molasses, @ 75¢ ; 50 lbs. Sugar, @ 12¢ ; 12 lbs. Coffee, @ 11¢.

6.—Sold Stephen O. Hayward, on %, 1 brl. Mess Pork, $11 ; 3 boxes Sugar, ea. 500 lbs., @ 6¢.

7.—Bo't of J. B. Atwood, Bill of Mdse., as per Invoice, $300 - - - - - Gave in payment order on S. O. Hayward for $101 ; Balance on %, $———.

8.—Sold James Sweeney, on %, 100 lbs. Loaf Sugar, @ 9¢; 50 lbs. Crushed Sugar, @ 8¢ ; 3 hhds. Molasses, @ $20.

10.—Sold F. R. Stebbins, on %, 1 tierce Rice, 1800 lbs. @ 3¢.

SET II.

St. Louis, April 1, 1879.—Invested Cash, $1500 - - - - - Paid for Stationery, Postage Stamps, etc., $8 - - - - - Bo't of Roberts, Rhodes & Co., N. Y., on %, Mdse. per Invoice, $4000 - - - - - Sold James Campbell, on %, 10 yds. Calico, @ 12¢ ; 5 yds. Ribbon, @ 20¢; 20 yds. Sheeting, @ 10¢ ; 5 yds. Broadcloth, @ $3. - - - - - Received cash for sales this day, per tickets, $115.25.

2.—Paid for Insurance, ½% on $4000, $20; for Drayage on Mdse., $5 - - - - - Received for sales this day, per tickets, $175.

3.—Sold Lauren G. Thomas, on %, 15 yds. Cassimere, @ $1; 20 yds. Dress Silk, @ $1.25 - - - - - Drew out for personal expenses, $15 - - - - - Paid porter on % of wages, $5 - - - - - Rec'd cash for sales this day, per tickets, $87.23.

4.—Sold R. B. Finney, on %, 10 yds. Vesting, @ $5; Trimmings, etc., $10 - - - - - Paid expenses cleaning store, $2.50 ; Paid for 1 box Pens, 88¢ - - - - - Rec'd cash for sales this day, per tickets, $110.50.

5.—Sold David P. Johnson, on %, 6 yds. Flannel, @ 50¢ ; 12 yds. Alpaca, @ $1.50 - - - - - Sold Isaac Stevens, on %, 12 yds. Dress Silk, @ $1.50; 6 yds. Fine Broadcloth, @ $4 - - - - - Paid for Letter Press, $7.50 ; for putting light in window, $2.50 - - - - - Received cash for sales this day, per tickets, $183.25.

6.—Received cash on % of James Campbell, $10 - - - - - Paid clerk's salary, $15 - - - - Received cash for sales this day, per tickets, $100.

8.—Sold Cyrus Wheelock, on %, 25 yds. 10-4 Sheeting, @ 75¢ ; 6 pairs Ladies' Hose, @ $1 ; 12 yds. Printed Jaconets, @ 15¢ - - - - - Paid cash for 1 doz. balls Twine, $1.20 ; for Carriage Hire, $4 - - - - - Received for sales this day, per tickets, $215.

9.—Paid Drayage, $4; Porterage, $3; for Show Case, $20 - - - - - Received for sales this day, per tickets, $76.

10.—Sold Robert Demarest, on %, 25 yds. Black Doeskin, @ $2 ; 50 yds. Bleached Shirting, @ 15¢ - - - - - Paid for Safe, $250 ; Book-keeper on %, $10; Small items of expense, $1.28 - - - - - Received for sales this day, per tickets, $110.

11.—Paid rent in full to May 31, $200 ; on Bill of Furniture, $25 - - - - - Received for sales this day, per tickets, $76.75.

12.—Received from Cyrus Wheelock, cash on %, $15 - - - - - Sold James Atwater (per wife), on %, 1 doz. Linen Hdkfs. $6; 10 yds. Cotton Damask, @ 25¢ ; 14 yds. Black Bombazine, @ $1.50 - - - - - Received for sales this day, per tickets, $84.

13.—Received for sales this day, per tickets, $98.75.

15.—Sold James Campbell (per daughter), on %, 1 pair Lisle Gauntlets, $1 ; 12 yds. French Calico, @ 15¢ ; 3 doz. Satin Buttons, @ 25¢ ; 8 skeins Twist, @ 4¢ - - - - - Paid cash for Express charges, $1.50 ; for Postage stamps, $1 - - - - - Paid carpenter for repairing store, $56.83 - - - - - Received for sales this day, per tickets, $95.

16.—Sold James W. Lusk, on %, 1 yd. Black Satin, $2; Trimmings for Vest, $1.50 - - - - - Received for sales this day, per tickets, $88.75.

17.—Received from Robert Demarest order on S. S. Packard to balance %, $———- - - - - Received cash for sales this day, per tickets, $126.31.

18.—Paid cash for Drayage, $4; Freight, $7.50- - - - - Received for sales this day, per tickets, $175.

19.—Sold James Atwater, on %, 20 yds. Linseys, @ 50¢; 30 yds. Corset Jeans, @ 30¢; 1 doz. Gents. Socks, $3 - - - - - Received for sales this day, per tickets, $210.50.

20.—Sold S. S. Packard, 10 yds. French Broadcloth, @ $4; 50 yds. Globe Drills, @ 13¢; 20 yds. Paper Cambrics, @ 12¢; 15 yds. Cotton Damask, @ 25¢; 30 yds. Cottonades, @ 33¢; 6 pairs Kid Gloves, @ 75¢; Received cash on %, $50; Balance due, $——— - - - - - Received for sales this day, $112.81.

22.—Paid cash for 2 tons Coal, @ $5; Paid balance on Furniture, $53 - - - - - Received for sales this day, per tickets, $103.20.

23.—Received for sales this day, per tickets, $129.

24.—Received for sales this day, per tickets, $180.58.

25.—Sold John J. Howell, Jr., on %, 10 yds. Mixed Satinet, @ 75¢; 6 yds. Cotton Drilling, @ 10¢; 1 yd. Fine Satin, $2; 10 skeins Twist, @ 4¢ - - - - - Paid Book-keeper on %, $15 - - - - - Received for sales this day, per tickets, $98.

26.—Received for sales this day, per tickets, $163.75.

27.—Sold Amos Dean, on %, 6 yds. Black Doeskin, @ $2; 1 doz. Linen Hdkfs., @ 50¢ each; 6 pairs Gents. Hose, @ 25¢ - - - - - Paid cash for Drayage, $10; Porterage, $6 - - - - - Received for sales this day, per tickets, $173.81.

29.—Paid Express charges on package from Chicago, $1.50; Paid Freight on Mdse., $24.75 - - - - Received for sales this day, per tickets, $74.10.

30.—Received cash on % of James Atwater, $20; also of Lauren G. Thomas, in full of %, $——— - - - - - Received for sales this day, per tickets, $125 - - - - - Sold Isaac Stevens, on %, 14 yds. Poplin, @ $1.25; 1 pair Kid Gloves, $1.

May 1.—Sold James Campbell, on %, 12 yds. Brilliants, @ 25¢; 35 yds. Blk. Bombazine, @ $1.50 - - - - - Paid cash for firkin of Butter for family, $10.

2.—Sold R. B. Finney, on %, 10 yds. Blk. Doeskin, @ $1.63; 25 yds. Brown Sheetings, @ 12¢; 20 yds. Check Gingham, @ 20¢ - - - - - Paid cash for Stationery, $1.50.

5.—Paid Roberts, Rhodes & Co., on %, cash (per draft on New York), $2000.

6.—Sold S. S. Packard, on %, 15 yds. Duck Drilling, @ 20¢; 10 yds. Brown do., @ 30¢; 6 pairs Pearl Spun Hose, @ 75¢.

7.—Sold David P. Johnson, on %, 8 yds. Broadcloth, @ $4; 10 yds. Doeskin, @ $2; 1 yd. Satin, $2; Trimmings, $5 - - - - Sold Robert Demarest, on %, 14 yds. Dress Silk, @ $2 - - - - Paid clerk's Salary, $50 - - - - Received for sales this week, $497.84.

9.—Sold Robert C. Spencer, on %, 10 yds. Flannel, @ 50¢; 6 Linen Hdkfs., @ 38¢; 20 yds. Brown Sheeting, @ 12¢.

10.—Received of Isaac Stevens, cash on %, $30.

12.—Sold R. B. Finney, on %, 6 pairs Gents. Hose, @ 25¢; 1 pair Suspenders, $1; 1 pair Kid Gloves, 75¢ - - - - Paid cash for Invoice of Mdse., Freight, etc., $1575.88 - - - - Paid on % of rent, $50; for carriage hire, $15.

14.—Received for sales this week, $553.25.

15.—Sold James Campbell, on %, 10 yds. Broadcloth, @ $4; 6 yds. Doeskin, @ $2 - - - - Received cash on % of R. B. Finney, $25.

17.—Paid cash for ton of Hay, $12.

20.—Sold John J. Howell, Jr., on %, 4 yds. Beaver Cloth, @ $3; 1 yd. Satin, $4; Trimmings for Coat and Vest, $8 - - - - Paid Gas Bill, $10.24.

21.—Received of Cyrus Wheeler, cash in full of %, $_____ - - - - - - - - Received for sales this week, $723.85.

25.—Received of R. B. Finney cash to balance %, $_____.

26.—Paid for Postage stamps, $3; for Stationery, $5.

27.—Bo't of John J. Howell, Jr., on %, 2 cords Wood, @ $5; 50 lbs. Butter, @ 16¢ - - - - Sold James W. Lusk, on %, 13 yds. Mous. de Laine, @ 25¢; 14 yds. Figured Silk, @ $1.50; Trimmings for Dress, $10.

28.—Sold Robert C. Spencer, on %, 12 yds. Broadcloth, @ $4; 6 yds. Doeskin, @ $2 - - - - Received for sales this week, $573.24.

30.—Sold Amos Dean, on %, 50 yds. Brown Sheeting, @ 12¢; 10 yds. Pressed Flannel, @ 75¢ - - - - Received cash of Amos Dean in full of %, $_____.

INVENTORY: Merchandise on hand, $1075.45.

SET III.

Albany, July 1, 1879.—H. B. Bryant and H. D. Stratton commence business with the following resources—gains and losses to be divided equally. H. B. Bryant invests, Cash, $1200; Merchandise, as per Inventory, $4750; Notes, as follows: one dated June 7, @ 30 ds., for $500, signed by Robert Bruce, and endorsed by Henry Ivison, and one dated Jan. 10, @ 8 mos., for $1000, signed by S. S. Packard, and endorsed by Jas. W. Lusk; Personal Accounts, as follows: John R. Penn, $500; L. Fairbanks, $750; Alonzo Gaston, $375 - - - - H. D. Stratton invests, House and Lot, valued at $5000; Cash, deposited in Union Bank, $3000 - - - - Paid cash for Postage stamps and Pens,

$5 - - - - - Sold Robert Van Schaick, for cash, 110 yds. Merrimack Prints, @ 11¢ ; 75 yds. Union do., @ 10¢ ; 120 yds. Orange do., @ 9½¢ ; 80 yds. Lowell do., @ 10¢.

2.—Received cash, on %, of J. R. Penn, $250 - - - - - Paid cash for printing Hand bills, $10.

3.—Sold James Johnson, on %, 2 cases Men's Thick Boots, 24 pr., @ $2 ; 3 cases Calf Welt Boots, 36 pr., @ $3 ; 1 case Boys' Grain D. S. Boots, 12 pr., @ $3 - - - - - Received cash for petty sales, $17.50.

4.—Sold E. H. Bender, on his note @ 60 ds., endorsed by J. T. Calkins, 1 case Pemberton Remnants, 1200 yds., @ 5½¢ ; 9 pieces Lynn Cottons, 270 yds., @ 11¢ ; 3 pieces Scotch P. Ginghams, 125 yds., @ 10¢ - - - - - Paid C. Jones for repairing store, per check, $175.

5.—Bo't of Claflin, Mellen & Co. (N.Y.), on %, Invoice of Boots and Shoes, amounting to $575 - - - - - Bo't of A. T. Stewart & Co., on %, Invoice of Dry Goods, $757 - - - - - Paid Freight on Mdse., per check, $27.50.

7.—Sold E. B. Rice, on %, 2 pieces Eagle Cottons, 80 yds., @ 12¢ ; 3 pieces Garibaldi Twills, 95 yds., @ 9¢ ; 2 pieces Bleached Drills, 90 yds., @ 11¢ ; 4 pieces Marietta Cloth, 120 yds., @ 12¢ - - - - - Received of Alonzo Gaston, cash in full of %, $——— - - - - - Paid clerk hire in cash, $25.

8.—Sold W. H. Clark, for cash, 3 pieces Bar Muslin, 54 yds., @ 13¢ ; 2 pieces Brilliants, 64 yds., @ 20¢ - - - - - Traveling expenses to New York, paid in cash, $15.75.

10.—Sold Benjamin Payn, on %, 6 pieces Paper Cambric, 72 yds., @ 8¢ ; 1 piece 6-4 Cotton Damask, 36 yds., @ 40¢ ; 1 piece Canvas, 25 yds., @ 13¢ - - - - - Received cash for Robert Bruce's note, $——— - - - - - Paid A. T Stewart & Co., on %, $300.

12.—Sold Calvin S. Sill (Troy), on his note @ 90 ds., endorsed by G. V. S. Quackenbush, 10 pieces Fancy Linens, 120 yds., @ 25¢ ; 20 pieces Crash Linen, 200 yds., @ 9¢ ; 15 pieces English Prints, 200 yds., @ 22¢ ; 36 Balmoral Skirts, @ $2.25 - - - - Accepted P. R. Spencer's draft, @ 10 ds., on H. D. Stratton, for $75 - - - - - Received cash for petty sales, $33.50.

13.—Sold Amos Dean, on %, 3 cases Kip Brogans, 72 prs., @ $1.50 ; 2 cases Ladies' Sandals, 120 prs., @ 60¢.

15.—Gave Claflin, Mellen & Co. our note @ 60 ds., to balance %, $——— - - - - Paid H. B. Bryant, on private %, cash, $75.

16.—Received of Lorenzo Fairbanks, cash on %, $350.

18.—Sold George H. Doty (Schenectady), for cash, 2 cases Women's Walking Shoes, 120 prs., @ $1 ; 1 case Ladies' Morocco Shoes, 48 prs., @ $1.50 ; 4 pcs. Check Marseilles, 40 yds., @ 75¢ ; 10 pcs. Cambric Curtain cloth, 120 yds., @ 25¢.

19.—Paid cash for advertisement in *Evening Journal*, $15.

20.—Sold Victor M. Rice, on %, 1 doz. Silk Scarfs, @ 88¢ each ; 4 pieces English Tweed, 36 yds., @ $1.12 ; 2 pieces Spanish Check Prints, 80 yds., @ 40¢ - - - - - Received on % of V. M. Rice, $30 - - - - - Paid cash for petty expenses, $10.

21.—Received cash on % of Amos Dean, $50 - - - - - Paid Bill for Carpenter work, per check, $175 - - - - - Paid cash for Drayage, $5; for Postage, $3.

22.—Sold James R. Morgan (Buffalo), on his note @ 60 ds., endorsed by W. P. Spencer, 36 Elastic Hoop Skirts, @ $2.50; 12 Stella Shawls, @ $2; 6 pieces Parametta, 300 yds., @ 75¢.

23.—Sold James Shelden (Schoharie), on %, 3 cases Congress Gaiters, 36 prs., @ $1.30; 4 cases Jenny Lind Gaiters, 48 prs, @ $1.12; 2 cases Misses' Sandals, 96 prs., @ 33¢ - - - - - Sold Robert Metcalf, for cash, 4 cases Men's Thick Boots, 48 prs., @ $1.50; 3 cases Calf Welt Boots, 36 prs., @ $2; 1 case Patent Leather Boots, 12 prs., @ $5; 1 case Misses' School Shoes, 60 prs., @ 50¢.

24.—Sold Charles Heyden (Greenbush), for cash, 1 piece Black Doeskin, 20 yds., @ $1.25; 3 pieces Corset Jeans, 90 yds., @ 10¢; 6 pieces De Laine, 180 yds., @ 40¢ - - - - - Received of E. B. Rice, cash in full of %, $———.

25.—Sold William Shepard (Hudson), on %, 6 pieces Lancashire Gingham, 250 yds., @ 10¢; 1 piece Canvas, 30 yds., @ 12½¢; 1 piece Padding, 40 yds, @ 10¢; 3 pieces Wiggin, 60 yds., @ 8¢ - - - - - Sold Robert Dawes (Pittsfield, Mass.), for cash, 4 cases Misses' Fancy Ties, 96 prs., @ 70¢; 2 cases Ankle Boots, 48 prs., @ $1.25; 1 case Kid Gaiters, 24 prs., @ $1.50 - - - - - Paid clerk hire in cash, $25 - - - - - Paid cash for acceptance favor of H. D. Stratton, $———.

26.—Sold John Belden (Utica), on %, 2 pieces Fancy Cassimeres, 50 yds., @ $1.25; 3 do. Saco Cassimere, 60 yds., @ $1; 9 do. Hard Times Cassimere, 270 yds., @ 20¢; 2 do. Striped Satinet, 80 yds., @ 50¢ - - - - - Paid A. T. Stewart & Co., cash in full of %.

27.—Sold James H. Lansley, for cash, 12 Stella Shawls, @ $2; 36 Balmoral Skirts, @ $2.25; 24 Silk Scarfs, @ 88¢.; 36 Gents' Linen Hdkfs., @ 35¢.

29.—Sold Wm. H. Fiquet (Marion, Ala.), for cash, 8 pieces Turkey Red Prints, 200 yds., @ 16¢; 10 pieces English Tweed, 90 yds., @ $1; 2 do. Spanish Check, 80 yds., @ 40¢ - - - - - Received of John R. Penn, cash in full of %, $———.

31.—Sold Charles A. Seeley (Rochester), on %, 4 cases Misses' Renfrew Boots, 96 prs., @ $1; 2 do. Ladies' Rarey Boots, 24 prs., @ $2; 2 do. Misses' Union Gaiters, 48 prs., @ 80¢ - - - - - Received cash on above %, $75.

INVENTORY.

Merchandise,	-	-	-	-	$3000.
Real Estate,	-	-	-	-	5000.

SET IV.

Brooklyn, April 1, 1879.—James Lester and Robert Brown enter into copartnership this day, as Dealers in Furniture and Cabinetware, under the firm-title of "Lester & Brown," Mr. Lester transferring to the firm the Assets and Liabilities of a former business, and Mr. Brown investing an equivalent in cash, as per terms of contract - - - - - James Lester invests as follows: Mdse. (finished articles), per I. B., $3000; Materials and Unfinished Work, $2500; Tools and Implements, $300; Notes on hand, per Bill-Book, $1375; Balance of David Owens's %, $230; Bal. of Thomas Webster's %, $57.30; Bal. of Timothy Paywell's %, $175 - - - - - The Firm assume for him the following liabilities: Note favor of Joseph Wiggins, due Apr. 20, $500; Note favor of Peter Jones, due Sept. 10, $250; Balance due Austin Packard on %. $175; Balance due J. W. Bulkley, $230 - - - - - Robert Brown invests cash, $6482.30 - - - - - Paid cash for Stationery, $5; for Postage stamps, $3.

2.—Received from David Owens cash in full of %, $———— - - - - - Sold A. A. Low, Brooklyn, on %, 1 Rosewood Tête-à-tête, $60; 1 Gothic Mahogany Bedstead, $20; 6 Mahogany Chairs, carved, $25; 1 Marble-top Table, $15 - - - - - Sold H. W. Beecher, Brooklyn, for cash, 1 Dressing Bureau, Serpentine Front, $22; 1 Lounge for Study, $15; 1 Gothic Hall Stand, R. W., $24 - - - - - Paid J. Stevens & Co.'s bill, Box Lumber, $75 - - - - - Paid cash for Glue and Varnish, per Expense Book, $18.75.

3.—Sold H. W. Clark, Williamsburg, on %, 6 Cane-bottom Chairs, Mahogany, $15; 1 Black Walnut Tête-à-tête, $25; 1 Mahogany Centre Table, $14; 1 Mahogany Card Table, O. G. Front, $7.

4.—Received from H. W. Clark cash on %, $50 - - - - Sold J. J. Powell, Jamaica, on his note @ 30 ds., 1 Card Table, Mahogany, $8; 1 Sofa Table, B. W., $9; 1 Piano Stool, R. W., $7.50; 2 small Wash-stands, @ $2.50 - - - - - Sold Thomas Proctor, Yonkers, for cash, 1 French Bedstead, B. W., $15 - - - - Paid cash for J. White's Bill of Hair Cloth, $150.

5.—Sold J. W. Bulkley, Williamsburg, on %, 1 pair Ottomans, B. W., $10; 1 Lounge Brocatelle, $15; 6 Parlor Chairs, R. W., @ $5 - - - - - Paid cash for Copy Press, $6; for Letter Book, $2.

6.—Sold John N. Pattison, New York, for cash, 1 Piano Stool, $8; 1 Music Rack, $4; Paid Workmen wages to date per Time Book, $128.17.

7.—Sold Richard Bannister, Chester, on %, 1 Stuffed-back Chair, $15; 1 Cottage Bedstead, B. W., $12; 1 Gothic do., $20; 4 Parlor Chairs, Mgy, @ $4; 1 Corner Stand, $4 - - - - - Sold Henry W. Taylor, Brooklyn, for cash, 1 Double-leaf Secretary, $35; 1 Enameled Cloth Lounge, $10 - - - - - Received cash for John Simpson's note, $500.

8.—Sold T. L. Cuyler, Brooklyn, for cash, 1 Extension Dining Table, $14 ; 6 Kitchen Chairs, @ 50¢ ; 1 Book Case, R. W., $40 ; 1 Hall Stand, R. W., $15 - - - - - Paid Simpson's Bill for B. W. Lumber, in cash, $350.

10.—Sold Robert McGrath, Islip, for cash, 2 Quartette Tables, Mgy, @ $2.50 ; 1 Sofa Table, Lyre Front, $11 ; 1 Large Arm Chair, $12 ; 2 Sewing Chairs, Cane Bottom, @ $3.25 - - - - - Paid cash for Petty Expenses, per Expense Book, $15.30.

12.—Sold James Smith, Hempstead, for cash, 12 Dining Chairs, @ $1.50 ; 1 Dining Table, $15.

13.—Paid Workmen's wages, per Time Book, $121.33.

15.—Received from Thomas Webster cash in full of %, $———— - - - - Sold Roger Bacon, Haverstraw, on %, 1 Lady's Arm Chair, R. W., $10 ; 1 Lady's Sewing Chair, R. W., $7.50 ; 1 Card Table, R. W., $6 ; 1 Cabinet Box, R. W., $20 - - - - - Effected Insurance on Building and Contents, paid premium in cash, $85.

18.—Paid Austin Packard cash in full of %, $175 - - - - - Sold Wm. F. Turner, Brooklyn, for cash, 1 Single Bedstead, $6 ; 6 Cottage Chairs, @ $1.75 ; 1 Quartette Table, $5.

20.—Sold John Anderson, Brooklyn, on %, 1 set Enameled Furniture, $65 - - - - - Received from Richard Bannister cash on %, $30 - - - J. Wiggin's note, $500.00 - - - - - Paid Workmen's Wages, per Time Book, $113.17.

25.—Sold James E. Jenkins, Brooklyn, on his note @ 60 ds., 1 Sofa Bedstead, Patent, $45 ; 6 Parlor Chairs, Brocatelle, @ $5 - - - - - Received from Roger Bacon cash in full of %, $———— - - - - - Paid cash for Drayage, $10 ; for Postage stamps, $3.

27.—Received from Richard Bannister his note @ 30 ds. to balance %, $37 - - - - - Paid Workmen's Wages per Time Book, $121.

28.—Sold David Woods, Red Hook, for cash, 1 Tête-à-tête, B. W. and Broc., $40 ; 1 Easy Rocker, B. W. and Broc., $25 ; 1 Corner Stand, $4.00.

30.—Sold H. W. Clark, Williamsburg, on %, 1 Sofa Bedstead, Patent, $45.

INVENTORY TAKEN APRIL 30.

Value of Finished Stock,	-	- -	$4250.
" Unfinished Stock,	-	- -	1875.
" Tools and Implements,	-	-	500.

May 1.—Messrs Lester & Brown have this day associated with them Robert Lincoln, who is to make an equal investment with each of the two former partners, and share equally in gains and losses. The Books of Lester & Brown are therefore made to exhibit their Resources and Liabilities, each partner being credited with his share of the Net Gain, and the balances brought down as a new investment. The new firm is to be styled "Lester, Brown & Co." - - - - - Robert Lincoln

invests cash, $———— - - - - Sold Peter Jamieson, Morrisania, for cash, 1 " Sleepy Hollow" Chair, $18 ; 1 Enameled Bedstead, $20 ; 1 Enameled Washstand, $5 - - - - - - Deposited cash in Central Bank, $12000.

3.—Sold A. A. Low, Brooklyn, on %, 2 Gothic Chairs, B. W. Stuffed, $30 ; 1 set Enameled Furniture, $75 - - - - - Paid Sundry Expenses, per Expense Book, in cash, $18.75.

4.—Paid Fisher & Bird's Bill for Marble in cash, $115 - - - - - Paid Workmen's Wages, per T. B., $117.50.

5.—Sold Joseph Brooks, Bellvale, on %, 2 Cupboard Washstands, @ $6 ; 1 Hat Rack, $5 ; 1 Dining Table, $14 ; 1 Black Walnut Crib, $5 - - - - - Received of John Anderson, cash in full of %, $————.

6.—Sold J. W. Bulkley, Williamsburg, on %, 1 Centre Table, B. W. Carved, $25 ; 1 Bureau, Serpentine Front, $24.50 ; 1 Side " Whatnot," $4.50.

8.—Received of Timothy Paywell, cash in full of %, $————.

9.—Paid J. W. Bulkley, cash in full of %, $————.

10.—Sold Richard Bannister, Chester, on %, 1 Reclining Chair, patent, $12.50 ; 1 High Book Case, B. W., $40 ; 1 pair Footstools, $4.50.

11.—Paid Workmen's Wages per Time Book, $128.75.

15.—Sold C. L. Derby, New York, for cash, 1 set Enameled Furniture, $75 ; 1 Tête-à-tête, $30 ; 1 Rosewood Sofa, $60 - - - - - Paid sundry expenses, per Expense Book, in cash, $24.30.

18.—Sold Ivison, Phinney & Co., New York, for cash, 1 B. W. Library Book Case, $75 - - - - - Paid Workmen's Wages, per Time Book, $98.50.

20.—Sold W. L. Stimson, Penn Yan, for cash, 2 Plain Wash-stands, @ $2 ; 1 French Bedstead, B. W., $25 ; 1 single do., B. W., $10 ; 6 Dining Chairs, @ $1.50 ; 3 Parlor do., @ $4.50 - - - - - Paid L. Johnson's bill for Plush, etc., in cash, $124 - - - - - Sold Steamer Isaac Newton, North River, on %, 6 Rosewood Tête-à-têtes, @ $35 ; 24 Rosewood Chairs, @ $5 ; 3 Stuffed Brocatelle Arm Chairs, @ $25 ; 1 Carved Rosewood Centre Table, $50.

25.—Sold A. A. Low, Brooklyn, on %, 150 Orchestra Chairs, for Academy of Music, @ $4 - - - - - Paid Workmen's Wages, per Time Book, $113.75.

28.—Sold Geo. McDougal, New York, for cash, 1 Hall Stand, $4 ; 6 Parlor Chairs, @ $2.75 ; 1 Wash-stand, $10 - - - - - Paid sundry expenses, per Expense Book, $19.25.

30.—Sold Abraham Fuller, Jamaica for cash, 1 B. W. Sofa, $30 ; 1 Tête-à-tête, $25 ; 1 Large Dining Table, $16 ; 2 Gothic Chairs, @ $5 - - - - - Sold R. Van Norman, New York, for cash, 1 Piano Stool, $10 ; 1 Music Rack, $5 ; 3 Arm Chairs, Rosewood, @ $15.

INVENTORY, MAY 31

Finished Stock on hand, $4750 ; Unfinished Stock, $875 ; Tools and Implements, $500.

PART II.—SET I.

New York, January 1, 1879.—Bought of Smith & Sons, on %, 1000
    brls. Flour, @ $6.

    2.—Sold Robert Bates, for cash, 300 brls. Flour, @ $6.50.

    5.—Sold Peter Cooper, on %, 250 brls. Flour, @ $7.

    7.—Sold John Jones, on his note @ 30 ds., 150 brls. Flour, @ $7.

    10.—Bought of J. R. Wheeler, on our note @ 60 ds., 500 bush. Wheat,
        @ $1.

    12.—Sold James Turner, for cash, 100 bush. Wheat, @ $1.25 ; 100 brls.
        Flour, @ $6.75.

    14.—Paid cash for Stationery and Books, for use of store, $50.

    15.—Bought of Thos. Payne, for cash, 300 brls. Flour, @ $5.

    17.—Sold Patrick Murphy, for cash, 100 brls. Flour, @ $6.

    18.—Bought of Geo. Davis, on %, 1000 bush. Oats, @ 75¢.

    20.—Sold Raymond & Co., on their note @ 5 ds., 500 bush Oats, @ 80¢ ;
        100 bush. Wheat, @ $1.15.

    22.—Sold Abram Fuller, for cash, 400 brls. Flour, @ $6 ; 300 bush.
        Wheat, @ $1.10.

    25.—Bought of James Hathaway, on %, 1500 brls. Flour, @ $5.50.

    27.—Sold Jonas Clark, on %, 1000 brls. Flour, @ $6.

    28.—Received cash in full for Raymond & Co.'s note, $515.

    29.—Sold John Drummond, for cash, 500 brls. Flour, @ $5.75 ; 500 bush.
        Oats, @ 90¢.

    30.—Paid Clerk Hire, in cash, $50 ; Store Rent, $50.

SET II.

New York, February 1, 1879.—Commenced business this day with
    the following resources and liabilities taken from Ledger A. (*See
    Statement, page 121.*) RESOURCES : Cash on hand, $8270 ; Notes on
    hand, $1050 ; Peter Cooper's account, $1750 ; Jonas Clark's do.
    $6000 - - - - - LIABILITIES : Notes outstanding, $500 ; Smith & Sons'
    account, $6000 ; Geo. Davis's do., $750 ; James Hathaway's do.
    $8250 - - - - - Bought of Comstock & Co., for cash, 10 hdds. N. O.
    Molasses, 600 gals., @ 40¢ ; 10 do. Cuba Sugar, 9500 lbs., @ 5¢ ;
    17 bags Rio Coffee, 1575 lbs., @ 16¢ ; 20 half-chests Oolong Tea,
    1080 lbs., @ 50¢ ; 10 tierces Rice, 5000 lbs., @ $4\frac{1}{2}$¢.

    2.—Sold S. S. Randall, on %, 3 gals. Molasses, @ 50¢ ; 200 lbs Sugar,
        @ 6¢ ; 150 lbs Coffee, @ 16¢.

    3.—Sold James W. Lusk, on his note @ 30 ds., 2 hhds. Sugar, 2100 lbs.,
        @ 6¢ ; 10 half-chests Tea, 540 lbs., @ 55¢ - - - - - Paid cash to Geo.
        Davis, in full of %, $———.

4.—Sold Henry C. Spencer, on %, 2 hhds. Molasses, 120 gals., @ 45¢.

5.—Bought of J. A. Tilford, on our note @ 60 ds., 10 tubs Lard, 400 lbs.,
@ 13¢; 20 boxes Soap, 1400 lbs., @ 7¢; 5 brls. Pork, 1000 lbs.,
@ 10¢ - - - - - Sold Harmer Smith, for cash, 2 brls. Pork, 400 lbs.,
@ 10½¢; 1 tierce Rice, 500 lbs., @ 5¢.

6.—Sold B. F. Carpenter, on %, 2 tierces Rice, 1000 lbs., @ 5½¢; 1 bag
Rio Coffee, 150 lbs. @ 18¢ - - - - - Bought of Clarence Doubleday, for
cash, 10 brls. Potatoes, @ $3; 1000 lbs. English Dairy Cheese,
@ 18¢.

7.—Sold James Reed, for cash, 10 lbs. Coffee, @ 18¢; 3 boxes Soap,
210 lbs., @ 8¢.

8.—Bought of Robert Hanaford, for cash, 10 hhds. Havana Sugar,
11000 lbs., @ 5¢; 3 do. N. O. Sugar, 3700 lbs., @ 5½¢.

9.—Sold Henry Van Dyck, on %, 2 hhds. Havana Sugar, 1970 lbs.,
@ 6¢.

10.—Paid James Hathaway, cash on %, $4000.

12.—Sold James Hathaway, on %, 1 brl. Pork, 200 lbs., @ 11¢; 1 bag
Rio Coffee, 110 lbs., @ 18¢; 1 hhd. Havana Sugar, 900 lbs., @ 6¢.

13.—Sold L. Fairbanks, on %, 100 lbs. English Dairy 'Cheese, @ 25¢;
1 brl. Potatoes, $4.

14.—Sold Henry Van Dyck, on %, 10 lbs. Coffee, @ 18¢; 50 lbs. English
Dairy Cheese, @ 25¢; 50 lbs. Rice, @ 5½¢.

15.—Paid cash for Rent of Store, $100 - - - - - Sold J. T. Calkins, for cash,
150 lbs. English Dairy Cheese, @ 25¢.

17.—Received cash of Henry C. Spencer, in full of %, $————.

18.—Sold S. S. Randall, on %, 25 lbs. Tea, @ 56¢; 50 lbs. Lard, @ 15¢;
20 lbs. Rice, @ 5¢.

20.—Sold Peter Cooper, on %, 2 brls. Pork, 400 lbs., @ 11¢.

22.—Sold E. F. Hill, on %, 1 half-chest Tea, 54 lbs., @ 60¢.

23.—Received of Jonas Clark, in full of %, cash, $3000; Note @ 90 ds.,
$3000.

25.—Paid Smith & Sons, cash on %, $3000 - - - - - Sold Geo. Davis, on %,
2 hhds. N. O. Molasses, 120 gals., @ 44¾¢.

26.—Paid cash for our note, favor of J. R. Wheeler, $500 - - - - - Sold
E. C. Bradford, for cash, 10 lbs. Rio Coffee, @ 19¢; 10 lbs. Tea,
@ 50¢; 50 lbs. Rice, @ 7¢.

27.—Sold Edwin Morgan, for cash, 1 tierce Rice, 500 lbs., @ 6¢; 2 brls.
Potatoes, @ $3.

28.—Paid Clerk's Salary in cash, $100.

INVENTORY : Merchandise unsold, $2500.

[SET III SAME AS IN PART I.]

SET IV.

Chicago, September 1, 1879.—S. S. Packard, John R. Penn, and J. C. Bryant are partners. S. S. Packard invests, Cash, $5000 - - - - - J. R. Penn invests Merchandise, amounting as per Inventory to $6750. The firm assumes for him two notes—one favor of J. Mattox for $750; and one favor of Henry Brown for $1000 - - - - - J. C. Bryant invests: J. Smith's note for $750; H. Young's do. for $750 and personal accounts as follows: J. T. Calkins, $500; E. R. Felton, $376; J. H. Goldsmith, $1170; Jas. Atwater, $1250; P. C. Schuyler, $1104. The firm assumes for him personal accounts, viz.: Chas. Taylor, $500; J. W. Lusk, $400 - - - - - Paid cash for Postage stamps, $3 - - - - - Sold Theron W. Woolson, Mt. Pleasant, Ia., for cash, 4 doz. Shirts, 2d quality, 48, @ $1; 6 doz. Union Neckties, 72, @ 38¢; 20 doz. Linen Hdkfs., 240, @ 50¢; 3 pcs. Cassimere, 150 yds., @ $1.25; Disc. off, 5% - - - - - Sold Ira Packard, Peru, Ind., on his note @ 6 mos., 50 Boys' Overcoats, @ $5.50; 50 do., @ $7.50 - - - - - Received cash for petty sales, per P. C. B., $54.25.

2.—Received of J. T. Calkins, cash on %, $200 - - - - - Paid Chas. Taylor, cash on %, $300.

3.—Sold D. V. Bell, City, for cash, 1 Dress suit for self, $50; 1 Overcoat for son, $15; 1 box Hdkfs., 6 doz., @ $4 - - - - - Received cash for petty sales, per P. C. B., $28.90.

4.—Paid cash for 2 tons Coal, @ $5.

5.—Received cash for petty sales, per P. C. B., $105 - - - - - Sold J. H. Goldsmith, Detroit, 2 pcs. English Broadcloth, 100 yds., @ $4; 50 Military Coats, per order, @ $10 - - - - - Received cash for petty sales, per P. C. B., $105.

6.—Paid cash for bill of Stationery, $15; Paid hands, for shop work, $150.

7.—Sold James Allen, Dubuque, for cash, 20 Zouave Uniforms, @ $25; 1 piece Striped Satin, 50 yds., @ $5; Disc. off Satin, 5% - - - - - Paid cash for Invoice Cloths, per I. B., $3000.

10.—Received cash of Jas. Atwater, on %, $750 - - - - - Paid cash for Gas bill, $15.

12.—Sold Jas. Atwater, Madison, on %, 1 lot ready-made clothing, viz.: 10 Coats, @ $3; 20 do., @ $3.50; 50 do., @ $5; 8 prs. Pants, @ $3; 25 do., @ $4; 50 Vests, @ $1.50; 25 do., @ $3; 1 Overcoat, $15 - - - - - Received cash for petty sales, per P. C. B., $58.

13.—Paid hands, for shop work, cash, $175.

14.—Received cash for petty sales, per P. C. B., $138.

15.—Gave Jas. W. Lusk our note @ 30 ds. to bal. %, $———— - - - - - Sold Wm. Baker, Springfield, for cash, 5 doz. Cravats. 60, @ 75¢; 3 doz. do., 36, @ $1; 9 doz. Linen Hdkfs., 108, @ 50¢; Disc. off, 5% - - - - - Sold J. T. Calkins, North Bend, Ind., on %, 50 Military Coats (privates), @ $10; 5 do. (officers), @ $15 - - - - - Paid cash for our note favor H. B., and interest. Face of note, $1000. Interest to date, $46.75.

16.—Received cash on % of J. T. Calkins, $150.

17.—Received cash for J. Smith's note, and interest to date. Face of note, $750. Interest, $34.25.

18.—Sold C. D. Bragdon, Rock Island, on his note @ 6 mos., 50 Coats (ready-made), @ $5; 100 prs. Pants, @ $3; 50 doz. Collars, @ $1.50; 5 doz. F. Y. Shirts, 60, @ $1.75 - - - - - Received cash for petty sales, per P. C. B., $94.83 - - - - - Paid Clerk's Salaries in cash, $112.

20.—Received of P. C. Schuyler, his note @ 60 ds. to bal. %, $———— - - - - Sold Geo. E. Harvey, Green Bay, on his note @ 60 ds., 100 Zouave Uniforms, @ $20; 50 Military Coats, "Co. H," @ $10 - - - - - Paid cash to hands, for shop work, $250.

22.—Received cash on % of J. H. Goldsmith, $1000; for petty sales, per P. C. B., $112.44.

25.—Sold Jas. W. Lusk, City, 50 Uniforms ("Lincoln Green"), @ $25; 30 do. (Zouaves), @ $15 - - - - - Received of E. R. Felton, cash in full of %, $———— - - - - - Received for petty sales, per P. C. B., $83.75 - - - - - Paid Rent to Sept. 30, in cash, $100.

26.—Received of J. H. Goldsmith, cash on %, $170 - - - - - Received for petty sales, per P. C. B., $58.94 - - - - - Paid cash for Porterage and Drayage, $35.

27.—Received of Jas. Atwater on %, cash, $500 - - - - - Received for petty sales, per P. C. B., $117.50.

28.—Sold Robert McGrath, White Pigeon, 20 Boys' Coats (ready-made), @ $5; 30 Vests (ready-made), @ $1.50; 20 doz. Collars, @ $1; Disc. off, 5% - - - - - Received cash for petty sales, per P. C. B., $87.50 - - - - - Paid cash to hands, for shop work, $275.

29.—Received cash in full for H. Young's note. Face of note, $750. Interest accrued to date, $14.50 - - - - - Received cash for petty sales, per P. C. B., $112.94.

30.—Sold E. R. Felton, Peoria, on %, 75 complete Uniforms, @ $25 - - - - - Received cash for petty sales, per P. C. B, $175 - - - - - Partners' salaries for month, paid in cash, $606.

[For a continuation of this business, see page 181 (Fourth Series).]

MATERIAL FOR SHORT SETS.

EITHER IN SINGLE OR DOUBLE ENTRY.

The material furnished herewith is intended to supplement the regular sets of the main work—or to supplant such of them as may be deemed best. The transactions will be found specially useful for drill exercises, or examination tests.

Supplementary Set 1.

Carting Business.—Single Proprietorship.

New York, July 1, 1880.—Began business with a cash capital of $5000 ----- Bought for cash 4 horses, carts, and equipments, $800 ----- Paid cash for rent of stable, one month, $25.

July 8.—Received cash for cartage during the week, $75 ----- Work done on %, viz.: For W. A. Miller, $10; J. L. Hunt, $15; Thos. Hunter, $12 ----- Paid workmen's wages, $35.75.

July 15.—Paid cash for horse-shoeing, $7; For repairing carts and harness, $3.75 ----- Received cash for carting during the week, $83.75 ----- Work done on %, viz.: Thos. Hunter, $10; William Taylor, $17; J. L. Hunt, $3; C. E. Cady, $5.75 ----- Paid workmen, $29.50.

July 22.—Received cash for drayage during the week, $85 ----- Work done on %, viz.: Thos. Hunter, $15; W. A. Miller, $17.50; C. Claghorn, $18 ----- Received cash, viz.: W. A. Miller, on %, $18; Thos. Hunter, on %, $27; J. L. Hunt, in full, $——.

Horses, carts, and equipments, valued at cost.

Required the condition of the business, and the net gain or loss.

Supplementary Set 2.

Dry Goods Business.—Single Proprietor.

Albany, Sept. 1, 1879.—Began business with a cash capital of $1000 ----- Paid for repairing store, $75 ----- Bought goods of G. A. Crocker, New York, on %, amounting, per invoice, to $2517.

Sept. 5.—Sold Merchandise, viz.: To C. S. Sill, Troy, on %, for $175; To McCook, for cash, $210.30; To E. G. Folsom, on his note at 30 ds., $412.75.

Sept. 12.—Paid one month's rent of store, in cash, $100 ----- Paid employés, for services, $50 ----- Sold merchandise to Joseph Brower, on %, $317.25 ----- Received from C. S. Sill, Troy, goods, not as ordered, for which we credit him $25.

Sept. 30.—Settled with Joseph Brower for his indebtedness—accepting a compromise of 75%: Cash received, in full of %, $237.94; Lost the balance, $—— ----- Paid cash for petty expenses $17.50 ----- Paid G. A. Crocker, cash on %, $500 ----- Sold merchandise, for cash, $375.

Merchandise on hand, $1584.72.

Required a full statement of the business, as to property, condition, etc.

Supplementary Set 3.

Business of a Teacher.—SINGLE PROPRIETORSHIP.

Philadelphia, Oct. 1, 1879.—Began business with a cash capital of $1500 ----- Paid cash for furniture and implements, $750 ; For office-books and stationery, $50 ; For 5 tons of coal, $25.

October 20.—Received cash for tuition, $1500 ----- Paid janitor, $30.

October 30.—Paid cash for teachers' salaries, $120.

November 10.—Paid cash for 2 months' rent, $300 ; For repairs, $30 ----- Paid teachers' salaries, $90 ----- Paid janitor, $30.

December 30.—The following amounts are due for tuition, etc. ; From W. J. Carter, $53.75 ; From W. L. Hill, $73 ; From S. G. Howe, $89.50 ; From Rednor Wood, $115.30 ----- The following balances are due teachers : To Sallie L. Cook, $25 ; To Alice P. Luick, $57 ; To Geo. S. Bigelow, $100 ----- Paid janitor's wages, $30 ----- Paid for two months' rent, $300.

Estimated value of furniture and implements, $750 ---- Unexpired rent, $150.

Required a full statement of current and standing condition.

Supplementary Set 4.—*Continuation of Set 3.*

Business of Teaching.—COPARTNERSHIP.

[The business represented in the previous set is continued, under a copartnership, the new proprietor investing in cash an amount equal to the net capital shown at the close of the previous month. The partners in the new firm are, the previous proprietor (supposed to be the student, who will fill the blank with his own name) and Thos. M. Pierce, under the title of —— & Pierce.]

Philadelphia, January 1, 1880.—Thos. M. Pierce invests cash, $——— ----- Paid Sallie L. Cook, balance of salary due, $———.

January 4.—Received cash of Rednor Wood, in full of %, $——— ----- Received cash for tuition, $183.75 ----- Paid janitor, $15.

January 15.—Received cash for tuition, $517 ----- Deposited cash in Union Bank, $3500 ----- Paid cash : To Geo. S. Bigelow, on %, $50.

January 20.—Rec'd cash for tuition, $325 ----- Paid janitor's wages, $35.

Feb. 5.—Paid for repairs, $15.75 ----- Received cash for tuition, $175 ----- Paid balances due teachers : G. S. B., $50 ; A. P. L., $57.

March 10.—Rec'd cash for tuition, $225 ---- Paid for office stationery, $15.

March 30.—Received cash for tuition, $1525 ----- Paid rent in full to date, $300 ----- Quarterly tuition bills unpaid, viz.: S. G. Howe, $175 ; W. J. Carter, $75 ; W. L. Hill, $100 ; G. W. Brown, $117.

March 31.—Paid teachers' salaries, in full, $575.

Value of furniture and fixtures, $700.

Required the interest of each partner at the close of business.

PRACTICAL HINTS.

In the preparation of this book the author has kept in view the fact that in order to become a good accountant, the student should learn not only to *think for himself*, but to give his thoughts proper expression; hence the introduction of "Exercises" and "Examples," intended to throw him upon his own resources, and remedy the evils which attend the practice of copying. This feature must commend itself to the faithful teacher who is satisfied with no progress which is not real. The three qualities essential to success in Accountantship are, 1. ACCURACY; 2. NEATNESS; 3. DISPATCH; and these can be acquired only through *practice*. Instead, therefore, of omitting any of the practical Exercises, or passing lightly over them, they should be regarded as indispensable, and even additional exercises should be given by the teacher or self-imposed by the student. The limited space renders it impossible to carry out in detail, all the labor which actual business would require in the way of filling out notes, drafts, checks, etc., or to suggest appropriate forms for such letters and documents as would be necessary in conducting the business represented; but the student should be required to supply this deficiency, with such aid as the teacher may offer.

The following hints are submitted as appropriate.

ORDER AND NEATNESS.

There is no error more common than that a theoretical knowledge of general principles will prepare a person for the duties of the Counting Room. It is true that *without* this knowledge, one need never hope to succeed; and equally true that with no other knowledge the way will be very difficult. Although in enumerating the qualifications of an Accountant we have placed NEATNESS *second* in the list, it is the *first* which attracts attention, and is of the utmost importance in the practical work of accountantship. Neatness in book-keeping is the result of *good writing* and *tasteful arrangement*. It is a mistaken idea that the ability to form a few wondrous curves in the execution of capital letters or the adornment of a fancy title, constitutes the chief qualification of a business writer. Practical men do not usually appreciate such qualifications, but insist, rather, on the utmost modesty of display and simplicity of arrangement. A professional *flourish* is as much out of place on a page of business record, as a daub of paint on a marble statue. Uniformity, legibility, and adaptation to space and purpose should be the characteristics of business writing; and he who fails in these will need something more than a certificate from a professor of pen art to save him. These remarks are not in disparagement of any style or system of penmanship, nor designed to underrate the very useful profession which makes good writers; but to place the *practical* above the *fanciful;* and to insist upon a proper recognition of the standard of taste which business men have adopted. Rapidity of execution is an essential element in business writing, but even this should be subordinated to neatness. In the selection of script for the principal forms in Part I. reference has been had to the standard of neatness above indicated; it is not expected that the student will attempt to copy the *style* of the writing, but it is hoped that he may seek to emulate its legibility and taste in arrangement. Particularly should he seek to avoid errors which require erasures. Nothing so destroys the beauty of a page as erasures and interlineations. Even occasional *blotting* is preferable to occasional *scratching*. Where it is possible, errors should be corrected by counter entries, thus affording an explanation, without destroying the harmony of the page. Finally, let the student practice until he becomes proficient in *ruling*. In using red ink care should be had to keep it pure; and to that end, never use a pen that has been dipped in black. Even steel pens are thought to destroy the brilliancy of red ink, and quills are preferred on that account. A steel pen, however, is the best for ruling, and needs only to be kept perfectly clean.

PROFICIENCY IN MATHEMATICS.

The processes of book-keeping seldom call into practice the higher departments of mathematics; albeit a thorough mathematician—other things being equal—will make the best accountant. The kind of proficiency most available to a book-keeper is facility and accuracy in addition. The ability to add long columns of figures with speed and certainty is one of the very best claims a young man can present for a position of trust. So highly is this accomplishment esteemed by business men, that where it is wanting other qualifications sink into comparative insignificance. A clerk who "*never makes a mistake*" is sure of promotion and remuneration. There are many theories as to the surest and most rapid method of adding, and occasionally some eccentric genius electrifies the world with an exhibition of almost magical power in this direction; but the only thing that can with safety be relied upon is *practice*—faithful and continued *practice*. The student should be required to write down long columns of figures of various numerical values, and test his powers by adding, first in one direction and then in the other; occasionally trying two and three columns at a time. We give on the next page three simple processes of retaining the figure to be *carried*—a very important matter with beginners. The first is the usual method of writing the carrying figure *small* under the unit amount of the column which produced it. The second requires the addition of each separate column to be written down on a waste space commencing with the right hand column and carrying to the next as in the usual method; these separate amounts placed in their order, one under the other, will present in their unit figures, counting upward, the general result. The third method consists of the proper arrangement of the independent sum of each column, so that, being added, the proper result is secured.

EXAMPLES.

First Process.			Second Process.					Third Process.					
1829	25	1st column,	50									5	0
743	18	2d "	29							2	4	:	
2562	28	3d "	34						3	2	:	:	
145	19	4th "	39					3	6	:	:	:	
2823	25	5th "	39					3	6	:	:	:	
7574	28	6th "	19 994 90		1	6	:	:	:	:	:		
4291	83				1	9	9	9	4		9	0	
25	64												
19994	90												
333	25												

The process of adding two or more columns at once is much more simple than is generally supposed; requiring little, if any, more skill than the common method. The only point of difficulty is the necessity of adding units to units, tens to tens, etc. To give the student an idea of the process, we will take the two cent-columns in the above example, and add them together. Commencing with the lower amount, we proceed: 64 and 3 are 67, and 80 are 147, and 8 are 155, and 20 are 175, and 5 are 180, and 20 are 200, and 9 are 209, and 10 are 219, and 8 are 227, and 20 are 247, and 8 are 255, and 10 are 265, and 5 are 270, and 20 are 290; which is the sum of the two columns. It will be seen that we separate each amount into units and tens, adding the units to the units and the tens to the tens of the accumulating result. We will now vary the process by commencing at the top and adding downward; and also by adding the tens first: 25 and 10 are 35, and 8 are 43, and 20 are 63, and 8 are 71, and 10 are 81, and 9 are 90, and 20 are 110, and 5 are 115, and 20 are 135, and 8 are 143, and 80 are 223, and 3 are 226, and 60 are 286, and 4 are 290; the same result as before. By continued practice of this kind the student will soon astonish himself with his own proficiency. Let him practice on *two* columns, until he becomes thoroughly familiar with the process, and then take three, and four. The necessity of keeping his mind constantly on the alert for fear of adding tens to units, and units to hundreds, will serve to quicken his powers of concentration, and develop the practical resources of his mind.

TO DETECT ERRORS IN THE TRIAL BALANCE.

Undoubtedly the best method for guarding against the trouble of finding errors in the Trial Balance is *not to make* them; but as this advice is much more easily given than followed, and as, in despite of the best efforts, Trial Balances do frequently fail to balance, a few hints as to the best methods of discovering the errors may be kindly received. In the first place let it be remembered that while the Trial Balance is not a *sure test* of the correctness of the Ledger, no Double Entry Ledger *can be* correct that does not balance; hence, the necessity of knowing that the sides are equal. The Trial Balance is simply the summing up of the debit and credit sides of the Ledger to ascertain if they are equal. If the trial should prove that they are *not* equal, the cause must exist either in entries being omitted, posted to the wrong side, or in wrong amounts. A little observation will enable the accountant to classify the error under one of the above heads. If the precaution indicated in our first Double Entry sets be taken, viz.: to carry the total amounts posted into the Trial Balance—and either side agrees with the footing of the Journal columns, the difficulty is easily overcome, as the difference between the sides will show not only the error or combination of errors, but the *side* of the Ledger upon which they occur. For various reasons, however, it is not always convenient to embrace the total Ledger entries in the Trial Balance ; therefore for general purposes, we would suggest the following process for detecting errors: *First*, make sure that an error exists. It is often the case that an overweening anxiety to have the sides of the Trial Balance equal actually produces a *supposed* error, by dissipating the mind while engaged in ascertaining the result, and thus persistently, though erroneously realizing its own fears, by errors in addition. If an error *seems* to exist, before attempting to find it go carefully over the work of addition, proving it in every way. If the test should prove that the sides do not equal, refer to the Ledger accounts, and ascertain that the proper amounts have been transferred to the Trial Balance. Foot up the accounts very carefully, and permit no doubt to exist that the exact *condition* of the Ledger is shown in the Trial Balance.—*Second*, If the error still exists, ascertain its *exact amount*, and then look carefully for the same amount in the Journal, which may have been omitted in posting. If no such an amount should appear, or should not prove to have been omitted, next ascertain if any Journal Entry exists of *half* the amount, which being posted to the *wrong side* would produce the difference. Should this test prove unsuccessful, ascertain if the difference be divisible by 9, and if so, look carefully for a transposition of some amount posted.*—*Third*, Should this process fail, the last resort is to *check* the postings. First ascertain that the Journal entries balance and then go carefully over the work, checking in pencil mark, all entries that have been properly posted both on the Journal and the Ledger. The most reliable process of checking is to have one person take the Journal and call off the Ledger titles and amounts, slowly and distinctly—the debits first, and credits next—while another examines the Ledger entries to see if they correspond. Many practical accountants adopt the plan of thus checking before attempting to take a Trial Balance, for the purpose, not only of facilitating the labor but of being assured that the Ledger is absolutely correct. *We cordially commend the practice*, believing that if it is adopted, and faithfully carried out, there will be little need of resorting to any other method to ensure a balance. Above all, *let the student hunt up his own errors* of balance ; for while it is

---

* It is a curious fact that the difference between any given amount composed of two or more figures, and the same figures transposed, is divisible by 9. For example, the difference between 75 and 57 is 18; between 120 and 210, 90; between 195 and 159, 36, etc., all of which differences 18, 90, and 36, are divisible by nine, without a remainder. The illustration may be carried to any extent, with the same results.

true that all such errors are the result of carelessness, the adoption of means to detect them, will tend, in the greatest degree to perfect his mind in those practical questions and labor necessary to the full development of his powers. It is the duty of the teacher to open up to the pupil's mind the bearings of the various principles of the science he would inculcate, as well as to aid him in the application of those principles; but *practical results* should be the student's own work. For these he should be held responsible; and should never be allowed to fall into the loose habit of making errors that his teacher may find them.

RESOURCES AND LIABILITIES.

The student has been taught that certain Ledger accounts are used to show resources, and certain others to show liabilities, and that the correspondence between the resources and liabilities thus shown must agree, in a certain sense, with the accounts showing gains and losses. He must be aware, however, that all resources are not equally valuable; that, in the course of trade, persons may become indebted to us, both on note and on account, who will *never* pay; the resource thus represented being absolutely valueless. In estimating the condition of a concern, therefore, it is well to know whether the books are *truthful;* that is, whether the *resources* exhibited on their pages are absolute or fictitious. The importance of this precaution will be apparent when we consider that all gains in business, as shown by *business* accounts, are predicated upon the integrity of the resources. For instance, suppose we sell A. $500 worth of merchandise, and take his note for it. In recording the transaction, we credit Merchandise and debit Bills Receivable. In estimating our gains and losses, we, of course, include among the proceeds of merchandise this amount, which adds $500 to our gains. But suppose the note to be worthless. In this case Merchandise account is made to show a gain which does not exist. The error may be corrected by debiting Merchandise and crediting Bills Receivable, thus disposing of the matter at once. But suppose the real value to remain in doubt. The account may be worth its face, or 50% of its face, or nothing. In this case—and particularly if there were other accounts of the same character—it would be well to open a "Suspense" account, and credit it with an amount equal to the supposed deficiency, debiting Loss and Gain with the same. This would leave the doubtful accounts standing as *resources*, but being offset by Suspense as a *liability*, the question of value would be left to be determined by the final results. In either case, the account showing resource should be credited and Suspense debited. If payments of value are made, they will appear to the debit of some resource account and credited to Loss and Gain.

This method will be found preferable to that of closing doubtful accounts into Suspense; as it is equally effective in guarding against fictitious gains, and leaves the doubtful accounts undisturbed for a more satisfactory adjustment.

BUSINESS FORMS.

BILLS.

1. Produce.

NEW YORK, *Sept. 1, 1879.*

THOS. MAY PEIRCE,

Bo't of HALLIDAY & SMITH.

100 brls. Flour, "State Superfine" - - - @ $6.³⁰	630	
50 do. do. "St. Louis XX." - - - - " 9.⁵⁰	475	
110 do. do. "Western Extra," - - - " 6.⁴⁰	704	
	1809	
Rec'd Payment,		
HALLIDAY & SMITH.		

2. Groceries.

NEW YORK, *Dec. 13, 1879.*

C. E. CADY,

Bo't of H. K. THURBER & CO.

60 lbs. Granulated Sugar, - - - - - - @ 10½¢	6	30
100 do. Crushed do. - - - - - - " 12¢	12	
50 boxes Adamantine Candles, 143 lbs., - " 15¢	21	45
5 bags Porto Rico Coffee, 150 lbs., - - - " 16½¢	24	75
	64	50

3. Dry Goods.

SYRACUSE, *June 10, 1879.*

J. F. MOOAR & CO.,

Bo't of C. P. MEADS.

5 pcs. N. Y. Mills Sheetings, 72 in., 185 yds., @ 27½¢	50	88
3 do. Red Cross Cambrics, 96½ " " 8¢	7	72
10 do. Victoria Ginghams, 143 " " 28¢	40	04
1 do. Franconia Denims, 36½ " " 15¢	5	48
	104	12

RECEIPTS.

1. On Account.

$500.

CHICAGO, *May 4, 1879.*

Received April 30, 1879, Five Hundred Dollars, on account of Joseph H. Palmer.

H. B. BRYANT & CO.

2. In Full of all Demands.

$645.

ST. LOUIS, *Oct. 24, 1879.*

Received of E. P. Heald Six Hundred and Forty-five Dollars, in full of all demands.

W. M. CARPENTER.

3. To Apply on Contract.

$1000.

NEW YORK, *Aug. 16, 1879.*

Received of E. G. Folsom, One Thousand Dollars, the same to apply on contract for building house, dated May 1, 1879.

GEORGE W. LATIMER.

4. To Apply as an Endorsement.

$150.

PHILADELPHIA, *Mar. 4, 1879.*

Received on the within note, One Hundred and Fifty Dollars.

J. E. SOULÉ.

5. Receipt for Property.

ROCHESTER, *Apr. 28, 1879.*

Received of A. W. Randall, the following enumerated articles to be held in trust for him, and returned on his demand: one Gold Watch (hunting case), two Promissory Notes, each dated June 8, 1878, and signed by L. L. Williams—one for Three Hundred Dollars, due in six months from date, and one for Seven Hundred Dollars, due in one year from date.

THOS. H. SHIELDS

NOTES.

1. Individual Note.

$375.

UTICA, *Nov. 20, 1879.*

One month from date, I promise to pay to H. B. McCreary, or order, Three Hundred and Seventy-five Dollars, without defalcation, for value received, at Second National Bank.

JOHN R. CARNELL.

2. Joint Note.

$200.

NEW YORK, *July 1, 1879.*

Ninety days from date, we promise to pay to the order of L. S. Metcalf, at his office, Two Hundred Dollars, value received.

D. APPLETON.
CHARLES SCRIBNER.

3. Joint and Several Note.

$650.

BROOKLYN, *Aug. 17, 1879.*

Nine months after date, we, or either of us, promise to pay Henry A. Tidd, or order, Six Hundred and Fifty Dollars, value received.

A. S. GLADWIN.
H. K. MOTLEY.

4. Principal and Surety Note.

$300.

SAN FRANCISCO, *Feb. 6, 1879.*

For value received, on or before July 6, 1879, I promise to pay to the order of F. B. Clemmer, Three Hundred Dollars.

ALVA S. WALKER, *Principal.*
JAMES THOMPSON, *Surety.*

NOTE.—The usual form of a principal and surety note is for the principal to properly *sign* the note, and the surety to endorse it.

5. Note, Payable to Bearer (with interest).

$475.

KINGSTON, PA., *Aug. 1, 1879.*

Sixty days from date, I promise to pay W. L. Dean, or bearer, Four Hundred and Seventy-five Dollars, with interest from date.

L. L. SPRAGUE.

6. Non-negotiable Note.

$800.

BOSTON, *Jan. 4, 1879.*

For value received, I promise to pay to Ira Mayhew on demand, Eight Hundred Dollars.

D. T. AMES.

7. Chattel Note.

$900.

TRENTON, *June 17, 1879.*

Thirty days from date, for value received, I promise to pay to Arthur S. Gladwin, or order, Nine Hundred Dollars in " Thurber's Perfection " Flour, at the then market rate, the same to be delivered at the option of the owner within the limits of the city of Trenton.

JOSEPH BROUWERE.

DRAFTS.

1. Sight Draft.

$500.

BUFFALO, *Sept. 1, 1879.*

At sight pay to the order of A. H. Hinman Five Hundred Dollars, and charge to account of

C. L. BRYANT.

To W. P. GREGORY, }
  Newark, N. J. }

2. Time Reckoned from Sight.

$100.

EASTON, PA., *Jan. 2, 1879.*

At ten days' sight pay to the order of W. Blackman, at Citizen's Bank, One Hundred Dollars, value received.

J. L. KNAUSS.

To E. M. HUNTZINGER,
  Providence, R. I.

3. Reckoned from Date.

$175 20

MANCHESTER, N. H., *April 20, 1879.*

Ten days from date pay to James H. Lansley or order, One Hundred, Seventy five and $\frac{20}{100}$ Dollars, value received.

G. A. GASKELL.

To H. E. HIBBARD & Co., }
  Boston, Mass. }

DUE BILLS.

1. For Cash Drawing Interest.

$250.

WASHINGTON, D. C., *June 15, 1879.*

Due Henry C. Spencer, on demand, Two Hundred and Fifty Dollars, with interest from date.

ZALMON RICHARDS.

2. For Merchandise, without Interest.

$1000.

BROOKLYN, *Aug. 17, 1879.*

Due R. M. Bartlett or order, One Thousand Dollars, payable in wheat at market price, on the first day of October next.

CHARLES CLAGHORN.

ORDERS.

1. To Apply on Account.

$45.

BALTIMORE, *Oct. 15, 1879.*

Messrs. E. Burnett & Co. will please pay to the bearer Forty-five Dollars in merchandise, and charge the same to my account.

F. H. CASPARI.

2. In Full of Account.

$50.

NEW YORK, *April 13, 1879.*

C. E. CADY, Esq.:

Please pay to H. C. Wright, or bearer, Fifty Dollars in goods, and this shall be your receipt in full of my account.

WM. ALLEN MILLER.

CHECKS.

1. Payable to Bearer.

$150.

NEW YORK, *March 18, 1879.*

SECOND NATIONAL BANK.

Pay to..............*Jonathan Jones,* or bearer, *One Hundred and Fifty*....................... Dollars.

A. W. RANDALL.

2. Payable to Order.

$200.

NEW YORK, *May 9, 1879.*

EAST RIVER NATIONAL BANK.

Pay to...................*Byron Horton*..................or order, *Two Hundred*.................. Dollars.

S. S. PACKARD.

3. Certificate of Deposit.

$845.

PHILADELPHIA, *Nov. 14, 1879.*

KEYSTONE NATIONAL BANK.

Thos. M. Peirce has deposited in this Bank, Eight Hundred and Forty-five Dollars, payable to J. E. Soulé or order, on return of this certificate.

(No. 406.)

ALEXANDER H. SMALL, *Teller.*

SET OF EXCHANGE.

1.

Exchange for £500.   NEW YORK, *July 5, 1879.*

Ten days after sight of this my *first* Bill of Exchange (second and third of same tenor and date unpaid), pay to S. S. Packard or order, Five Hundred Pounds sterling, value received, with or without further advice.

T. A. EDISON.

To BROWN BROTHERS & CO., }
    Bankers, Liverpool.   }

2.

Exchange for £500.   NEW YORK, *July 5, 1879.*

Ten days after sight of this my *second* Bill of Exchange (first and third of same tenor and date unpaid), pay to S. S. Packard or order, Five Hundred Pounds sterling, value received, with or without further advice.

T. A. EDISON.

To BROWN BROTHERS & CO., }
    Bankers, Liverpool.   }

3.

Exchange for £500.   NEW YORK, *July 5, 1879.*

Ten days after sight of this my *third* Bill of Exchange (first and second of same tenor and date unpaid), pay to S. S. Packard or order, Five Hundred Pounds sterling, value received, with or without further advice.

T. A. EDISON.

To BROWN BROTHERS & CO., }
    Bankers, Liverpool.   }

ACCOUNT SALES.

Account Sales of 2000 Bush. Canadian Club Wheat, on % and risk of C. P. Meads, Syracuse.

1879					
June	18	C. L. Stewart on %,			
		1500 bush. @ $2.35 - - - - $3525			
"	20	G. C. Cannon, cash,			
		500 bush. @ $2.40 - - - - 1200	4725	
		_____CHARGES._____			
May	17	Freight and Drayage - - - - - - $325			
June	20	Storage, Ins., etc. - - - - - - - 17 26			
		Government Tax - - - - - - - 5 91			
		Commission 2½% on $4725 - - - - 118 12	466	29
		C. P. M.'s net proceeds - - - - - - -	$4258	71

BYRON HORTON & CO.

NEW YORK, *June 20, 1879.*